The Impossible Five

IN SEARCH OF SOUTH AFRICA'S

MOST ELUSIVE MAMMALS

Justin Fox

JACARANDA

This edition first published in Great Britain 2017
Jacaranda Books Art Music Ltd
27 Old Gloucester Street,
London WC1N 3AX
www.jacarandabooksartmusic.co.uk

Originally published in South Africa 2015 by NB publishers,
a division of Media24 Boeke (pty) ltd,
40 Heerengracht, Cape Town, South Africa

A CIP catalogue record for this book is available from the British
Library

ISBN: 978-1-909762-55-8
eISBN: 978-1-909762-56-5

Cover design: Michiel Botha
Jacket design: Jeremy Hopes

Printed and bound in the UK
by Jellyfish Solutions, Hampshire, SO32 2NW

In fancy they pursue
The dream-child moving through a land
Of wonders wild and new,
In friendly chat with bird or beast
And half believe it true.

From *Alice in Wonderland* by Lewis Carroll

CONTENTS

NOT THE BIG FIVE

Like most children, I grew up with stories of animals. Fairy-tale animals, dream animals, intelligent domestic animals and dangerous, toothy, wild animals. Members of my family took turns reading me to sleep at night. There were the *Barbar the Elephant* books and Dr Seuss's *Cat in the Hat* tales, Richard Scarry's heroic characters epitomised by the intrepid Lowly Worm, Beatrix Potter's world of erudite rabbits, books of African folktales and Kipling's *Animal Stories*. Winnie the Pooh and his coterie were favourite bedtime companions, and today I'm still able to recite whole chunks of A. A. Milne. Who can forget Piglet meeting a Heffalump, Eeyore losing his tail or Pooh getting his head stuck in a honey jar? These are indelible moments in my literary upbringing. I remember odd but important details, like the fact that Tigger had trouble climbing down from trees because his tail kept getting in the way. For years, I wondered if real tigers experienced the same difficulty.

Perhaps the book that most captured my imagination was *Alice in Wonderland*. The story of her adventures down the rabbit hole seemed to my young mind completely believable. Lewis Carroll's characters—the March Hare, Cheshire Cat and White Rabbit—inhabited my suburban playground as much as they did that enchanted college garden in Oxford, the setting for his famous book, written in the 1860s. Wonderland could be discovered anywhere. I eventually arrived in Oxford to study English many years later, and was thrilled to finally set foot in that charmed Christ Church garden.

When I was big enough to read for myself, weightier tomes such as *Watership Down, Jock of the Bushveld* and Gerald Durrell's animal escapades took over. I also began reading African tales of myth and legend, where I was never exactly sure whether the white lions, giant snakes and talking apes I read about were fictional characters or adaptions of flesh-and-blood animals. Real creatures and imaginary ones morphed into one. It was probably impossible to meet a real Pooh bear, but probably just as impossible to meet such a creature as an aardvark. Or was it?

Growing up in the city, my contact with animals was mostly domestic. We had two dogs and a cat, as well as a parade of smaller fry that passed through the house, or hid in the attic, or flew away, or floated belly-up in a bowl. I loved my cat Ling best of all. He was an intelligent and indulgent Burmese of impeccable breeding, who played games with me every day after school and slept on my bed each night.

Human children are, in a way, imprinted by their pets. That languid, cat-walk stride, the bored, eyes-half-closed, don't-bother-me-I'm-thinking-about-Nietzsche look—I grew to know such things in Ling intimately. I realise now that my love for Ling led me to an understanding, an affection even, of his movements and moods; the way he purred, or stretched after a snooze, or stalked a bird with his slow-motion gait. And so it was that when I eventually met bigger cats in the wild, there was an immediate, electric recognition. The love was already there.

When I was old enough for malaria tablets and able to sit still for longish periods without making a fuss, my parents started taking winter holidays in the game reserves, in particular the Kruger, South Africa's biggest national park on the border with Mozambique. Whenever we set out, the excitement was unbearable. This was a real-life, adult Wonderland, just as alluring and outlandish as Alice's. A hundred kilometres before arriving, I'd already have unpacked the binoculars, Roberts bird book and foolscap pad with three columns marked mammals, birds, reptiles.

The challenge was always to find the Big Five. On most Kruger holidays, we managed the first four: elephant, rhino, buffalo and lion. It was always the leopard that eluded us. After countless unsuccessful attempts, finding the spotted cat became something of an obsession for me. It was not until adulthood that I saw my first wild leopard, iconically draped on the branch of a leadwood tree beside the Sabie River. There was a jolt of recognition... and elation. It felt like a benediction. Ling had long since passed into the forests of the night sky by then, but I knew the set of those limbs, those steady golden eyes, the sinuous beauty as if they belonged to a long-lost friend.

As an adult, I continued the childhood tradition of exploring game parks each winter. Then I joined a travel magazine and started visiting reserves almost every month on assignment. I began to see tourists' relentless pursuit of the Big Five as one-dimensional. There was so much more out there, unseen, waiting to be discovered. After a dozen lion sightings, coming upon an African wild dog or a honey badger held more allure. My taste broadened and my passion for the wild in all its forms deepened. I now sought rarer animals: little-brown-job birds, strange insects and shy night creatures such as bush babies, civets and genets.

Over the years, my list of new creatures to find grew longer. There was one particular animal that replaced leopards on my most-wanted list: the pangolin. I'd heard a lot about these armadillo-like, prehistoric-looking mammals, and hoped to see one for myself. Each time I visited a game reserve, I'd ask the rangers about pangolins. Invariably they'd shake their heads and tell me to give up. "Impossible," they'd say. Most rangers had never seen one themselves, even those who'd spent a lifetime in the bush. My career as a travel journalist took me to parks all over Africa, but the story was always the same.

This fruitless search for pangolins got me thinking about creating a list of the mammals I'd tried and failed to find over the years; those animals you had just about zero chance of seeing. Instead of the Big Five, I would try to find the Impossible Five. After much deliberation, I narrowed my search down to a shortlist that included such animals as the black-footed cat, Cape fox, aardwolf and Knysna elephant. The last on this list was discounted after I found out there were probably less than five left in the Garden Route forests of the southern Cape, therefore my chances of finding them were nil, and these elephants were not a subspecies or genetic variant, but simply common-or-garden *Loxodonta africana*. I also considered a number of smaller, critically endangered African mammals, including four species of moles and two species of bats. However, my final five were all distinctive, sexy mammals that had long frustrated me (and my friends, family and many rangers I had spoken to). My Impossible Five would be: Cape mountain leopard, aardvark, pangolin, riverine rabbit and (naturally occurring) white lion.

These animals have survived into our modern age largely due to their elusiveness. Their "impossibility" is their tenuous insurance against extinction. They are still wild and free, most of them living outside national parks, occupying the same territories they have for millennia. As such, they are symbols of the wilderness that was once everywhere, but which is now drastically curtailed and shrinking by the day. Their continued presence, even if never seen, can be a comfort, a kind of ecological money in the bank. If they disappear or are driven into contained environments, our human species will be far poorer for it. I began to think of my creatures' impossibility as their saving grace—*our* saving grace. In this light, it didn't matter if I found none of them and my mission was a complete failure. As long as I knew—we knew—they were still out there, that would be enough.

I laid out a large, photocopied map of South Africa on my dining-room table. With a pen and highlighters, I marked the areas that were likely to prove fruitful in my hypothetical hunt. Now that I could see the project, visualise the months of searching ahead, it began to solidify into something with proper weight. The distances were vast, the terrain difficult, the chances of finding the animals slim. And yet... and yet the idea would not let go of me. It started to eat into my sleeping hours. All five animals took up residence in the burrows and branches of my mind and would not be dislodged. I realised, quite suddenly, that I was actually going to have to do this thing. It was the notion of having a choice in the matter that had been dislodged. A whimsical idea had turned itself into an imperative, and a bullying, all-consuming one at that.

My quest, or series of journeys, was going to be a costly business. As a journalist, I'd been working in and around Africa for more than a decade and could call on some of my old contacts and squeeze the odd favour. I approached magazines and websites, as well as a vehicle manufacturer (Land Rover) and various safari lodges, to help with logistics. In return, they'd get coverage in the print media and online, and there was also the dangled carrot of a probable book with the catchy title *The Impossible Five*. I contacted scientists and researchers working in the field, describing my quest to them in detail, explaining how it had become an obsession and how badly I needed to find these five animals. To my astonishment, every person I contacted said they would help. I told them that I might have to come and stay with them and hang around and become a nuisance while waiting for the animals to show up. And they still said yes. As each block fell into place, my excitement grew. I set aside six months: one mammal per month, with a month to spare. In the end, this quest would take me nearly three years.

Before setting off on the first journey, I took a closer peek at each of my five contenders. The Cape leopard is smaller and more elusive than its larger cousins elsewhere in Africa, and far rarer (more so, even, than Asia's snow leopard). Its territory lies in the mountain ranges to the north and east of my hometown, but it is hardly ever seen, and precious little is known about the last remaining big cats living so close to Cape Town. In a sense, these mysterious creatures have become an emblem of the old Cape—a Garden of Eden thronging with big game before European settlers arrived.

I'd been reading a lot of Bruce Chatwin, one of my favourite travel writers. His books, especially *In Patagonia* and *The Songlines*, were part of the reason I'd chosen my career. I was fascinated by his tantalising, unfinished writings about Africa, nomadism and the origins of our species. He contends that leopards are a reminder of our very distant past, when we were still ape creatures and nights were ruled by the spotted cat that hunted us in the dark. This notion led him to ask in *The Songlines* whether *Dinofelis*, the ancestral leopard, "was a specialist predator on the primates?... Could it be... that *Dinofelis* was Our Beast? A Beast set aside from all the other Avatars of Hell? The Arch-Enemy who stalked us, stealthily and cunningly, wherever we went? But whom, in the end, we got the better of." Perhaps in our subconscious, we humans still recognise who is really the Prince of Darkness, the prince of *our* darkness.

Aardvarks and pangolins are not as rare as Cape leopards, but just as hard to find. The aardvark is an improbable, but adorable creature with bunny ears and a Hoover snout. It looks as though evolution should have knocked it off the branch long ago. But somehow it persists, largely due to its elusiveness and nocturnal habits. The pangolin, with its prehistoric armoured scales and shambling gait, occupies a similar terrain, and has nocturnal habits and an insectivorous diet similar to the aardvark. My best chance of finding these two creatures was by making a trip to the Kalahari Desert, which straddles the Northern Cape and our two neighbours, Namibia and Botswana.

Lions are kings of the bushveld, members of the Big Five, and have no place on an impossible list such as this. However, white lions are a different story altogether. At the time I began my research, it was thought that there were only a handful of naturally occurring white lions in the wild, and these could be found in the Timbavati region of South Africa's Limpopo Province, adjacent to the Kruger National Park. But these cats moved through vast territories, so I was going to have to be on standby for months, ready to hop on a plane and follow up one of the rare sightings.

The riverine rabbit is officially the most endangered mammal in Africa, and the thirteenth most endangered on Earth. This little creature was probably going to be my hardest nut to crack. To make matters worse, there appeared to be precious little information about it. I tried to do some background reading, but soon gave up. My fauna bible, *Southern Africa's Mammals* by Robin Frandsen, was disconcertingly scant on detail: "Little known, solitary rabbit... Gestation period: unknown. Mass: unknown. Life expectancy: unknown. Spoor: unknown. Length: 43 cm." That's an awful lot of unknowns. At least I knew precisely the length of the creature I'd be looking for on the interminable nights that lay ahead, driving the dirt tracks of the Little Karoo in search of a nondescript bunny.

I opened my journal and wrote: "Riverine rabbit: 43 cm." Then I closed the book. It was time to pack the car and take to the road on a magical quest of miracle and wonder to find the Impossible Five.

THE UNSPOTTED LEOPARD

Tyger Tyger, burning bright,
In the forests of the night
("The Tyger" by William Blake)

Quinton Martins is mad. Not in some superficial, mildly nutty way, but rather his is a deep and abiding insanity. Quinton Martin is obsessed. There's no telling when his madness began but his obsession began in 2003 with the idea of finding the Cape mountain leopard. Most Capetonians know they exist—their tracks are occasionally found in the mountains, and every few years, to much public consternation, a farmer kills one—but no-one ever actually *sees* them. As such, they half-exist, occupying a place at the borders of public mythology and reality.

Quinton began looking for the elusive cat in the Cederberg, a mountain wilderness two hours north of Cape Town. For weeks at a time, he'd hike alone in the remoter parts of the berg (mountain), searching for any

11

sign—evidence of a kill, spoor or scat—of leopard. From there, his passion grew into a master's thesis and then a doctorate. He poured all his time and money into finding the cat. Sometimes lugging a backpack filled with sixteen cameras high into the mountains to set up camera traps with infrared sensors. A week or two later, he'd return to retrieve the film (there were only thirty-six shots to a roll) and set the traps in new positions. He took the film to his local camera shop and eagerly awaited its development. Not a single leopard showed its face. Quinton's disappointment and frustration grew. There were countless rolls of blank film strip, or shots of small, unremarkable mammals. This went on for months, until one day he was in the camera shop and, as usual, idly asked if the latest batch had any photos of cats.

"Ja," said Zelda, the shop assistant. "I think there's a nice one of a spotted kitty."

It was as though Quinton had stuck his finger in a light socket. Before he was fully aware of his actions, he'd vaulted the counter and run through to the back room. Sure enough, his camera trap had captured the image of a male leopard, destined to become M1, the first in a long line of cats that would consume Quinton's life.

It was nine months before he glimpsed his first leopard, and another year before he caught and collared one. He ran out of money and sold everything, including his car, to keep the fieldwork going. He had to hitchhike from Cape Town to the berg and do his research on foot, covering thousands of kilometres in the mountains with temperatures well below freezing in winter and as high as

47°C in summer. He carried no tent, just an old sleeping bag. When it snowed, he sheltered in caves or rocky overhangs. Madness.

Since childhood I, too, have had a thing for leopards, the most elusive of the Big Five. I remembered all those fruitless searches with my parents in the Kruger Park and how I'd craved to see a leopard more than any other creature. Now I wanted to meet Quinton and hopefully one of his spotted friends.

Driving up the N7 one spring morning, wild flowers lined the highway through the Swartland, the undulating wheat country north of Cape Town. The road led up over Piekenierskloof Pass towards the ramparts of the Cederberg, home to Quinton and his leopards. After the orange orchards of Citrusdal, I took the Algeria turn-off and crossed the chattering waters of the Olifants River on a causeway. This is the symbolic entrance to the most beautiful mountain range in Africa.

I stopped and got out to drink from a stream fringed with white sandbanks. Before me stood Grootberg's ochre buttresses, the mountain's main portal. The road snaked between slabs of Table Mountain sandstone towards a rocky gorge set in the clouds, each ridge leading me higher and deeper, past Algeria, over Uitkyk Pass and finally into the lovely, sequestered Driehoek Valley, the floor covered in sedges and marshes, the walls with boulders and protea bushes.

I was now in the heart of the Cederberg Wilderness area, 71,000 hectares of mountainous terrain, impossibly rich in fynbos flora and home to the rare and endangered

Clanwilliam cedar tree and snow protea. This alpine fastness is still frequented by smaller wildlife such as grey rhebok, klipspringer, honey badger, caracal, Cape fox, porcupine and Cape clawless otter, while raptors such as black eagle and jackal buzzard circle in the thermals overhead. The streams are home to the richest variety of endemic fish south of the Zambezi, most of them endangered. The prettiest of these is the Doring fiery redfin. With its sleek, spotted body and scarlet fins, it looks like a cross between a leopard and a daisy.

The Cederberg's allure is enhanced by its long human history. These mountains were once the realm of San hunter-gatherers, and possess a wealth of rock art stretching back at least 8,000 years. This is, in fact, the Lascaux of the Cape. Some of its most famous paintings, such as the iconic rain elephants—a row of ochre pachyderms thought to be a rainmaking site of shamans—are found at the Stadsaal rock formation, close to where I would be staying.

I'd booked a cabin on Driehoek Farm, and brought along enough provisions for a lengthy spell of self-catering, which for me means lots of barbecuing, so my vehicle was essentially full of wood and meat. A farm road led to a cluster of buildings, some thatched and whitewashed in the Cape manner, loosely arranged around a green commonage. Sheep filled a field, a vineyard clung to the slope and the battlements of the central berg rose up on all sides. It was ruggedly idyllic. A pack of dogs, led by a white Labrador, bounded up and escorted me to reception. We passed an inflamed male turkey, ogling a dowdy female and gobbling appreciatively. He made a valiant attempt to mount her, but she was having none of it. The Labrador barked encouragement while I knocked on the door. It was opened by Lizette Du Toit, the farmer's daughter. As she signed me in, we got chatting about leopards.

"Farmers used to set gin traps to kill predators, but with Quinton around things have changed a lot," she said. "You must ask him about Houdini, the old leopard that took fifteen of our sheep. My dad wanted him dead."

Lizette told me that Driehoek was established in 1832, making it the oldest farm in the Cederberg; it has been in the Du Toit family for five generations. She showed me a selection of their wines, whose grapes came from some of the highest vineyards in South Africa. I was given a map, and she pointed out a number of walks on the farm and adjacent valleys.

"Have you ever seen a leopard?" I asked.

"Ag, I've seen Max, our big male, a couple of times in my life, but these cats are helluva difficult to spot. Good luck!"

She directed me to a cabin that lay a long way down a farm track in a stand of poplar and oak trees, still leafless up here in the cold alpine air. A few empty caravans stood marooned like upmarket shacks in the campsite. My accommodation was a wooden, open-planned affair half encircled by large boulders and a dry-stone wall that dated from the 1800s. Out front a tea-coloured stream slipped through the reeds; beyond lay the serrated foothills of Sneeuberg, stepping away in stony ridges towards the skyline. Behind my cabin stood the squared-off monolith of Tafelberg, towering above the farm.

The heater was on in my room, despite the sunshine. It was going to be bitterly cold at night. My provisions were stacked on the counter: boerewors sausage and lamb chops, a bottle of plonk, packets of crisps, chocolates, spaghetti and pesto in a jar. I hadn't finished unpacking when I heard a vehicle pull up outside.

A tall figure wearing a floppy hat and spectacles arrived on my veranda, stomping the dust off his boots. "So, you ready to bag a leopard, then?" asked Quinton.

"Sure!" I said.

"Good, let's go set some traps."

Quinton was dressed from head to toe in sponsored gear. He had a web of crow's feet in the corners of his eyes, no doubt from years of staring at the sun-bleached landscape that hid his elusive cats. We climbed into his Land Cruiser, called Witblits (Firewater), which was branded with stickers from a host of sponsors, including the rather appropriate Leopard's Leap Winery. The words "Cape Leopard Trust", of which Quinton is the founder and project manager, were emblazoned on the driver's door.

"We couldn't keep the Trust going without sponsors," said Quinton as we bounced through the campsite. "But the bloody vehicle manufacturers won't give me a thing. Their 4X4s are carving up the landscape, and they're too miserly to help with a project aimed at protecting the environment. Bastards."

He chuckled. "It's not just sponsors we want.

Volunteers, too. Speaking of volunteers, I just need to make a quick stop and say hi to a retired couple helping me out. They're monitoring the transmitters on two traps I've set in the valley."

We pulled up beside a caravan parked in a glade of oak trees a few hundred metres upstream from my cabin. An older, balding man emerged from the tin igloo.

"No luck, Quinton, I've been checking every hour." Garth was a cheerful fellow who carried a chestnut-fronted macaw on his shoulder. She chimed in with a loud squawk. "Oh, she's such a clever girl. Wants to be involved in everything, don't you Gracie, even chasing after big kitties." The green bird ran its head up and down Garth's chin, to the man's obvious delight. He scratched his little friend's head with a practised forefinger.

"She was abused as a chick before we got her," said a pink-track-suited Lorraine, emerging from the caravan. "Now she only loves Garth. So possessive over him. Doesn't like women at all, not human ones anyway." She sounded a bit miffed at having been usurped by a bird. "But you've at least learnt to poop on command, haven't you Gracie?"

The bird cocked its head.

"Poop, Gracie, poop," said Garth dotingly, directing her tail away from his shirt. "It's better that she poops out here and not in the caravan or on me."

"It brings good luck, you know," said Lorraine, trying to sound enthusiastic.

"I'm not sure how much more good luck I can handle," said Garth.

"Maybe good luck turns bad if you get pooped on too many times," quipped Quinton.

"Oh no, it's always good luck if it's from Gracie," said Garth.

"Anyway, better be going," said Quinton. "We'll take the receiver and give you a few hours off duty."

As Quinton pulled away, we could hear Garth and Lorraine saying "poop, poop, poop" and Gracie calling after us "bye, bye, bye".

"Such a nice couple," said Quinton. "They've volunteered to sit here next to a receiver for a week, just waiting for the signal to change, which tells us a trap has been sprung. Without folks like them, our organisation couldn't function."

As we drove up the valley, Quinton told me about the Cape Leopard Trust. By 2004, he'd run out of his savings, and it looked as though the research would have to be abandoned. Then a local farmer, Johan van der Westhuizen, invited Quinton to come and see him in his office in Cape Town. Johan asked him to explain the project in minute detail. The farmer was so impressed, he handed over a cheque.

"That cash injection allowed me to keep going," said Quinton. "Our first leopard, M1, was named Johan."

His research soon led him to the conflict between humans and animals, and his focus began to shift. He felt strongly that leopards were being killed or relocated unnecessarily. That's when the idea of a predator conservation trust came about. Fundraising events were held and money started coming in. The programme grew and was extended into other parts of the Cape. Today, there are leopard projects running in the Boland mountains, Namaqualand and the Gouritz region.

"The biggest threats to the Cape leopard are habitat loss, persecution and disease," said Quinton, dodging a protruding root that lay python-like in the road. "It's only through long-term research over decades that we can truly understand what affects the population. To see the big picture, we'll also need to do ancillary projects on the leopards' principal prey, such as dassies and klipspringers."

Quinton explained that his board of trustees comprised eminent scientists, businessfolk and conservationists. Apart from various leopard projects, the work of the Trust included a comprehensive genetic analysis, which would determine if Cape leopards formed a unique genetic unit or subspecies. Solutions to human-animal conflict were being sought through scientific research, empowering farmers and local communities, as well as encouraging eco-tourism and running education programmes. Quinton took a right turn down a track that was closed to the public. The vehicle bounced over boulders like an inebriated frog.

"I first became interested in leopards while tracking them on foot at Londolozi Game Reserve in the greater Kruger Park," continued Quinton. "After a few years working as a field guide, I decided to study again and ended up doing zoology at the University of Cape Town. During varsity holidays, I came hiking in the Cederberg and started to notice leopard tracks. Farmers told me about the problems they were having with leopards, but no-one I spoke to had ever seen one. I discovered there was hardly any research on them at all. It was an ideal opportunity.

"There's something special about these particular cats. They're such elusive, ghost-like creatures. To me, they represent this incredible wilderness so close to Cape Town. I used to have up to six leopard sightings a day when I was a ranger in places like South Luangwa in Zambia. But here it's a massive challenge. You never see them. But they are here. If they were easy to spot, they'd all have been killed long ago.

"I initiated the research project and funded it myself. We started getting sightings and then began trapping. My best encounter was in a remote gorge on the eastern, Karoo side of the berg. It was a tough hike to get in there. I was busy setting up a camera station next to a river when I heard a leopard vocalising close by. It's an unmistakable rasping sound. You never hear that here. I thought the leopard might be coming along the path, so I hid a little way up the slope.

"Then I heard the vocalising *right* below me in a riverine thicket. I scanned the bushes with my binoculars. Nothing. Lowering my binocs to get a broader perspective, I saw a tiny movement out the corner of my eye. Slowly I turned my head and there she was, peeping around a rock and staring at me, about eight metres away. She had this absolutely perplexed look on her face: *what the hell is this thing?*

"I slowly moved my hand to my camera and she

watched its progress intently. I raised this crappy digital point-and-shoot, pressed the trigger and poof, she was gone. It's so isolated back in those valleys, there's a good chance she'd never seen a human in her life before. What a privilege, man, what a privilege."

The track petered out and the going got rougher. We crossed a river, drew to a halt beside a large boulder and got out. Before us was a scene suggestive of a slaughterhouse. A grysbok hung upside down from a hook hammered into the rock, its stomach slit open, blood dripping from nose and mouth. Heads and limbs of various animals lay scattered about. The stench was overwhelming.

"The grysbok is road kill," explained Quinton. "The other body parts are offcuts from an abattoir."

He pointed out the invisible trap. Sticks and bushes had been arranged so there was only one easy way to reach the suspended buck. Quinton checked the foot-loop snare while I stood at a distance trying to control my nausea. Once he'd checked and reset the trap, we headed on foot up Uilsgat Gorge along a path used by F10, also known as Spot, a female leopard that frequented the valley. Quinton carried a backpack with trapping paraphernalia, which included a mallet and a number of metal stakes. The sun was low and we moved in and out of icy shadows. I realised I should have brought a jacket.

We passed a second trap, right in the middle of the path. A red flag and signs warned people to keep clear. "I've asked CapeNature to close this area to the public," said Quinton. "Hikers are such a pain. They don't read the notices. Or, if they do, the buggers come and snoop around, triggering the snare. They're clueless."

I was about to mention that leopards could simply read the warning signs and avoid the area, but realised it was my childhood imagination—where literate cats were the norm—intruding.

Quinton was looking for a suitable place to set another trap. As we headed further up the path, I noticed that he had, almost imperceptibly, begun to change. His gait was somehow different, his body slightly hunched. He seemed more alert, more twitchy, stopping often, looking at the path with a cocked head. Thinking like a leopard?

"Here, this is the place," he said at last, lowering his backpack and taking the spade I'd been carrying. He dug a square hole, levered a foam base into position and laid the trap over the top. It comprised a simple foot plate with a trip and spring fastened to a wire noose that would tighten around the animal's paw. The wire was thick and smooth so as not to hurt the cat. It was attached to a bungee cord so the leopard's yanking would not break a limb. Quinton taped over any rough areas on the wire and cleared all stones and sharp sticks in the immediate vicinity so the creature couldn't wound itself as it thrashed about trying to extricate a paw. He carefully set the spring and attached a transmitter. The contraption was secured with long metal stakes driven into the ground by a mallet. It was imperative that a leopard be prevented from breaking free and heading into the hills with a trap attached to its leg.

"Aren't these snares just like the wire ones set by poachers?" I asked through chattering teeth.

"Similar. It's actually a more effective and safer method than the cage traps we used to employ. Animals picked up more injuries trying to force their way out of the cages. As long as we get to them soon after the trap is sprung, wire snares are okay. That's why the transmitters have to be monitored at all times."

He showed me how to set up a transmitter and how, as soon as the magnetic connection was severed, it began sending an altered signal. The volunteers at Driehoek would then call Quinton on a satellite phone and he'd race to the trap. If there was indeed a leopard caught, rather than a red-faced hiker, he'd phone the nearest vets, who were on permanent standby and could be there within two hours to dart the animal. A collar would then be fitted, measurements taken, and tissue and whisker samples extracted for DNA analysis. The cat would also be weighed, its age determined by teeth colouration and wear, and its general condition assessed.

Once fitted with a GPS collar, the animals could be tracked around the clock. Quinton was gathering valuable information from the data downloaded in the process. During the period of his PhD research, he'd managed to trap and collar thirteen leopards, and had gained considerable insight into their movements, diet and habits.

"Where did you catch your first one?" I asked.

"It was on Driehoek farm in August 2005," he said, pushing back his floppy hat and wiping the sweat from his forehead. "We'd been trying to get him for three months. His name was Houdini, and for good reason. By that stage I was already nearly two years into my research, and had not yet had a proper, close encounter with a leopard. Houdini had been nailing sheep throughout the valley, but I convinced the farmers to give me a chance at nabbing him. That cat was a sly one. Eventually we lured him with a sheep carcass, but he escaped from the first trap. We reset it and caught him a week later. Again, he escaped. It took another five weeks before we finally got him."

Once he'd finished preparing the trap, Quinton arranged his camouflage and subterfuge devices. By now, I was so cold I was having to bounce up and down to keep the blood circulating. Quinton ignored me as he covered his contraption with sand. This couldn't be done with a tell-tale human hand, so soil was sifted through a colander and sprinkled over the snare. Next, he cut foliage and planted it in a manner that would lead a leopard into the trap. Sticks were laid to encourage the cat to assume a particular stride and place its paw in exactly the right spot. Quinton got down on his hands and knees, head to one side, staring sceptically at the trap. He raised his front paw a little, hesitated, then adjusted a twig. If you narrowed your eyes, you could almost see his spots. Crawling a few paces on all fours, he slunk into the trap, all but triggering the snare on his wrist.

"The data we've been collecting can be used to alleviate conflict between farmers and predators," he said, morphing back into semi-human form. "We need to understand the role of predators in eco-systems. The Cape Leopard Trust is actually more about broader environmental conservation. We're using leopards as our flagship species for a much bigger project."

By now I was hugging myself to keep warm and I could feel my lips turning blue. If I didn't ask any more questions, maybe he'd hurry up, stop acting like a suspicious leopard and take me back to my snug cabin.

"You see, many farmers, and even the Department of Agriculture, ignore the fact that when you kill the apex predators, others simply move in. If you do somehow manage to eliminate all of them, another species will fill the gap and could bring with it even bigger problems. For instance, if you knock off all the leopards in one area, you might get a population explosion of dassies. The apex predators keep everything in balance. So the future must be about livestock management, not predator destruction."

"Gets a bit ch-ch-chilly up here when the s-s-sun goes down," I spluttered.

"Are you getting cold?"

"I-I-I think—"

"Look, we need to maintain functioning eco-systems." Quinton wasn't interested in my discomfort. "The Trust is conducting experiments with sheep farming in the Northern Cape. We're using trained herders and special dogs. The herders gather all sorts of info on both the livestock and the predators. This way we can make farming more scientific and offer concrete results to the naysayers."

"Um, I think I m-m-might need to head back to the ve-ve-ve-hicle before hypothermia sets in."

"We want to do more studies on baboon, caracal and jackal. Also klipspringer and dassie, to see how the whole eco-system fits together. And to find ways of alleviating farmer-predator conflict."

I began swinging my arms around like a windmill, hoping centrifugal force would return some blood to my hands.

At last Quinton was done. He stood up, brushed the sand from his knees and took off his heavy-duty gloves. Apart from the red flag and warning signs, it was impossible to see that the path hid a trap. Quinton loaded the remnants of the equipment into his backpack, handed me the spade and we trudged back down the valley. Ahead of us, the sun's last rays illuminated Tafelberg. Its highest bastions glowed in gaudy shades of salmon; the rest of the valley was sunk in shadow.

Quinton dropped me back at the cabin and headed to his home deep in the mountains at Matjiesrivier. I donned three extra layers and lit a barbecue fire. The wind was sniping and low clouds poured in from the west over Middelberg. I opened a bottle of workmanlike Shiraz and sat beside the fire staring at the living darkness. There was no moon and the stars hissed quietly in the icy firmament. The stream grumbled loudly, wind whooshed in the bare branches, the mountains pressed closer. Somewhere nearby was my leopard, up there among the crags, perhaps hunting, perhaps taking refuge from the elements beneath an overhang. Maybe she was watching me.

Sitting beside the pyramid of flames, I thought about

how the Cape mountain leopard has become a creature of legend and a symbol of what the Cape has lost. Three-and-a-half centuries ago, when Jan van Riebeeck stepped ashore to found his little settlement to grow vegetables for scurvy-ridden sailors of the Dutch East India Company, the peninsula had teemed with game. Cape Town itself was home to the Big Five. There were leopards on the crags of Table Mountain, buffalos and rhinos grazing the marshlands of Green Point, lions in the suburb of Oranjezicht and elephants browsing beside the city's streams, while the grunt of hippos echoed around the city bowl. It was an Eden of almost unimaginable bounty.

Settlers and farmers soon began to clear the land. The hippos of Cape Town's rivers were among the first to be shot. By the end of the twentieth century, there was not a single member of the Big Five left on the peninsula. The slaughter of large game continued throughout the Western Cape. In most places, only the names remind us of what we have lost: Zeekoevlei (Hippo Lagoon), Buffels Bay (Buffalo Bay), Renosterveld (rhino vegetation), Leeukloof (Lion Gorge), Olifants River (Elephant River). Most prevalent is the name "tier" or "tyger", as early Dutch settlers, unfamiliar with African fauna, called the leopards they encountered "tigers". Travelling among the mountains of the Cape, it's never long before you come across a Tygerberg or Tierkop, a Tierberg or Tierkranskop. Of all the Cape's free-roaming game, it was these secretive creatures that would have had the best chance of surviving into the twenty-first century. Their ghostly presence in the mountains fringing the city represents the last vestige of the rich diversity of wildlife we have lost.

After a meal of wors, chops and potato in a skin of tinfoil, I climbed into a bed piled with blankets. Sleep came quickly... and I found myself dreamily stumbling along a track in the mountains.

There was no moon to light the way, only a softening of the darkness that marked a sandy path. I grew frightened. The crags breathed danger. Crickets filled the night with ominous stridulations. There was a presence, something watching me. Perhaps the spotted night cat, Prince of Darkness? My path snaked into a narrow gorge beside a stream. Tall reeds leaned in from either side. The ground was soggy underfoot; my legs grew leaden. I passed beneath a cedar tree and paused. Thick boughs blotted out the stars. Fear gripped me. I could not take another step. Looking up, I saw a shape draped on a branch above my head. A pair of golden eyes bored into mine. His lips were parted and I could make out the glint of fangs. What beauty, what lethal grace. I was transfixed. *Tyger! Tyger! Burning bright, in the mountains of the night.* He was all power and sinew and dark fire, a work of art crafted by some immortal hand. He stared at me for what seemed an age, each second torn from the flesh of time. Then a wide grin spread across his face.

"Which way should I go from here?" I asked timidly.

"That depends on where you want to go," said the leopard.

"So long as I find my impossibles," I said.

"An aardvark lives in that direction," he pointed a claw

to the north. "A riverine bunny in that direction." He waved vaguely to the east. "But, my boy, they are both absolutely impossible to find." The leopard closed his eyes and rested a chin on those mighty paws. His body began to dissolve, leaving only his wide, Cheshire grin hanging in the air. I walked on into the night, tingling with excitement.

The rusty hinges of the guinea fowls' call woke me early, followed by a spell of utter silence. I got up and looked out the window. The ground was white with frost. The mountains were colourful cut-outs against a dark-blue sky. A hadeda ibis strutted about, drilling the lawn with its beak. After I had breakfasted on muesli and cold boerewors, Quinton arrived to collect me. We picked up Garth and Lorraine, and headed down the Driehoek Valley in search of Max. Gracie the macaw agreed to stay behind and hold the fort: her biting tongue would scare off most intruders. Except, perhaps, a spotted cat.

Quinton soon picked up a strong signal coming from the male leopard's collar on Sneeuberg, the 2027-metre massif to our right. Fortunately, he had a key to a private gate which let us onto a forestry track that wound up the side of a valley towards the peak. We crossed a stream and ploughed through tall vegetation, its fingers brushing the sides of the 4X4. The track grew steeper and rockier. On a rise above us stood a line of iconic cedar trees, highly endangered and probably on their way to extinction. Prone to fire and ruthlessly felled for timber in the twentieth century, only a few specimens of this endemic species cling on in the high berg.

A pair of black eagles circled above us like patrolling aircraft, ominous shapes etched against the sky. Like leopards, they are apex predators of the mountains, and there's no love lost between cat and bird as they compete for the same prey. Whenever eagles get the chance, they dive-bomb leopards to scare them away from their territory.

We came to a stop at what looked like a stone igloo beside the track. There was a narrow entrance and a metal sliding door that could be triggered to drop like a guillotine and imprison a creature inside. It was a sinister contraption, casting a shadow over the beauty around us.

"This is an old leopard trap," said Quinton. "All the farms in the area used to have them. Some are more than a hundred-and-fifty years old. Once the creature was caught, you could shoot it from above through gaps in the stonework. Farmers knew exactly where to place these things. So I've put quite a few of my own traps around here and had good success."

He went on to explain that gin traps are still used extensively throughout South Africa to eliminate "problem animals". Thousands of these nasty devices litter the rural landscape. They are indiscriminate, brutal and kill or maim far more innocent animals than rogues. Usually made of metal with saw-tooth jaws, the traps can sever a paw or ensnare the wounded animal long enough for it to starve to death.

"We are making progress, though, especially in the Cederberg. I've persuaded many farmers to change their methods, for instance, by introducing Anatolian sheep dogs. They're a far better deterrent than traps."

Then something caught Quinton's eye. "Look there!" he exclaimed, crouching next to the track and pointing at a vague indentation in the sand. He took out a tape measure. "Paw print. Six-and-a-half centimetres. Female. I'm sure it's F11. We haven't caught and collared her yet, so she doesn't have a proper name."

We walked a little way up the slope, following the spoor. Quinton pointed at the ground again. It was scat. It's difficult for lay people to fathom the excitement animal droppings induce in zoologists. Quinton fell to his knees like a worshipper and studied the specimen. He explained that usually only half the scat is taken for analysis, as it serves as a territory marker for leopards. Samples are soaked in formalin, washed, and the hair separated from other remains before being oven dried at 60°C.

Then the analysis can begin. To identify prey, the hair length and colour are noted, as well as cuticular hair-scale patterns. The presence of bone fragments and hooves also aids identification. Small rodents are trickier, although teeth found among the remains can help. Quinton explained that through scat research, he'd recorded twenty-three species in the diet of these opportunistic feeders, including everything from lizard to cow. I thought of the many hours Quinton must have spent soaking faeces in formalin, baking them and then the days spent analysing the contents. Dedication such as this must surely be fed by a singular brand of obsession.

We pressed on up the pass, creeping along the mountain face on a hairline track that led us into a world of jumbled sandstone and bright green fynbos. Clouds cast giant dapples across the valley below. All the while, the bleating transmission from Max's collar grew more intense. At the top of the pass, we got out and Quinton aimed his VHF telemetry at a nearby hill. The signal was strong. He switched to a UHF aerial and got a GPS fix from the collar. Max was eight-hundred-and-fifty metres to the west, just this side of a tall ridge. The four of us spent a few minutes scanning the area with binoculars, but saw nothing. Every bush and boulder looked vaguely feline. Every element in the landscape seemed ideal camouflage for a leopard.

"Okay, we're going to have to hike in after him," said Quinton. "It could get a bit rough."

The two retirees opted out; they said they'd rather sit and watch the view. Out came folding chairs and a flask of coffee. Knowing a wild-goose chase when I saw one, I half-wanted to join them. But I'd come to the berg to bag a leopard, and this was as good a shot as any. Hats, water bottles, telemetry, binoculars—we were good to go.

Ahead of us lay difficult terrain: a salad of rocks that had been sliced and diced into uncomfortable shapes. Quinton set off at a cracking pace. My lack of fitness became painfully apparent about a minute into our pursuit. Quinton has long legs and is used to pursuing feline quarry in the mountains. I have city legs, made for strolling the promenade as far as my local coffee bar. Quinton was like a Zen walker who never seemed to actually touch the ground. His leather Caterpillar hooves were like wings; my old hiking boots like anchors. I puffed and wheezed in his wake. Where his strides propelled him over gaps, I found myself caught between them. While his breathing remained even, I sounded like a steam engine.

He crouched behind a pile of stones up ahead. I made a last push, using all my reserves of strength to catch up. He glanced back with a frown and put a finger to his lips. I flopped down beside him, heaving like a turtle that had just lugged its body up a beach. I was as red as a tomato, and sweat was pouring off me. Quinton might have had a drop of perspiration on his brow.

We had covered at least four-hundred, near-vertical metres. He poked the telemetry aerial above the ledge like a periscope. Max had to be very close.

There was no signal whatsoever, only a hissing sound. "Shit, the bugger's gone over the edge," whispered Quinton. "Might have got wind of us. Come on!"

We were off again, bounding up the slope to the next ridge line. The weather had begun closing in. Low clouds scudded through gaps in the berg. The wind turned icy and the towering Sneeuberg dissolved into white. It began to rain. Quinton was pulling ahead once more. I watched him stop and stare at the terrain, head to one side, thinking like a cat again. Which way would Max have gone? Then the half-man, half-leopard slunk over a rise and disappeared.

After thirty minutes we reached another ridge line. I collapsed gasping next to Quinton, lungs wheezing. My thighs were incendiary and my right knee, the dickey one, had sort of capitulated. My vision was all spots and floaty hallucinogens. A leopard could have been standing two metres away, and I'd have dismissed it as retinal malfunction.

Quinton raised his telemetry aerial. "I've got a faint signal. Could be bouncing off the cliff. Max is heading west. He's missioning. We'll never catch him. This is the eastern most part of his range. He could be gone for weeks now, prowling his territory along the western slopes of the berg. It's completely inaccessible. I'm sorry."

We headed back, making a detour to a spot where Max had recently made a kill. All that remained was a sprinkling of klipspringer fur, which had been carefully removed and discarded by the leopard, and a reeking pile of stomach contents. Everything else had been consumed.

"From the data we got off his GPS collar, we know Max spent about twenty-four hours on this antelope carcass," said Quinton. "When we notice a GPS cluster in one particular spot, we come and investigate. These cats are so mobile that when they're stationary for a while, they're usually on a kill. But we missed him by about an hour. Such a sneaky fellow is our Max."

That evening, Quinton was due to give a talk on leopards at Mount Cedar, a popular lodge in a nearby valley. I got a lift with Garth and Lorraine to Quinton's Matjiesrivier home, a traditional thatched cottage leased from CapeNature, where he lives with his wife Elizabeth. She's a willowy woman with a mane of curly auburn hair and a Julia Roberts smile. Elizabeth used to be a Waldorf teacher in Stellenbosch. Now she runs environmental education and wilderness camps for children at Matjiesrivier. Their house serves as the de facto headquarters of the Cape Leopard Trust. The tall, creaky interiors are crammed with zoological books, pictures of big cats and maps of their distribution. It's the delightfully jumbled home of working scientists.

We transferred to Quinton's vehicle for the trip to Mount Cedar. Night was falling and the mountains were at their most seductive. As we drove, the rocks turned from gold to purple to burnished black, and stars began to prick the sky. Nearing the lodge, we breasted a rise and Quinton said: "This is exactly where I saw my first leopard. I'd been searching for nearly a year by then, and suddenly there it was, caught in my headlights. Just the briefest glimpse. Incredible."

He told us about his early searches in the desolate Karoo Cederberg to the east of the road we were driving. "It's the most isolated part of these mountains. No-one ever goes there. That's why I love it so much. You can walk for days and not see any sign of humans. Pure wilderness. I was in the leopards' environment, alone, sleeping wild. Occasionally I'd be backtracking along a route I'd just walked and there'd be fresh leopard spoor across my path. They knew all about my presence. I'd often hear other animals alarm-calling. I knew the leopards were close. But never so much as a glimpse. *Not* seeing them made it even more special, if you get my drift. The invisible cats. Like a fairy-tale."

We arrived at Mount Cedar for Quinton's 6.30pm presentation to a bunch of wealthy tourists. There were possible sponsors among them, so Quinton had been persuaded by the tour leader to do his "song-and-dance routine". But there was no-one in the auditorium, and Mount Cedar's dinner is served at 7 o'clock sharp. Quinton has to be a patient man, content to wait months for the glimpse of a cat. Now we witnessed his less patient side. There was, in fact, smoke coming out of his ears. He'd been specially asked to come as a favour. Dinner would just have to wait, or there'd be hell to pay.

Eventually a group of well-heeled guests sauntered in, chatting and laughing among themselves. There were carefully groomed women and blustery men, loud with bravado and bonhomie. I thought Quinton might lose his temper at their tardiness, but the moment he began his talk, he was charm personified, and the audience soon warmed to him. Elizabeth turned off the lights and images flashed on a screen. He'd done the PowerPoint presentation countless times before, and was completely at ease with his material.

We learnt how, after three-hundred-and-fifty years of farmer-predator strife, most of the Western Cape's wildlife biodiversity had disappeared. The last big cats, hanging on in a few scraps of wilderness, were all that was left. When Quinton founded the Trust in 2004, an average of eight leopards were being shot in the Cederberg each year. Since 2004, only two had been killed.

He explained that the Cape leopard was an iconic "umbrella species", used as an emblem for research on the entire eco-system and for environmental education. The tools of his trade were simple. Feet on the ground were the most important element, since much of the terrain was inaccessible by vehicle. Infrared-camera traps were vital, as they provided permanent eyes and could be used to identify individual leopards, their distinctive pattern of spots being the equivalent of a human fingerprint—no two exactly the same.

Quinton showed maps depicting the ranges of his cats. He'd found that in the mountains, male leopard ranges were up to two-hundred square kilometres, compared to the Karoo, where ranges were as high as 1200 square kilometres, or the densely populated Kruger National Park, where they were as low as twenty-five square kilometres. He'd recorded how ranges changed over time as cats were forced out or died. His leopards traverse up to thirty kilometres a day, patrolling their territory, hunting and looking for mates. Only one male at a time holds any given patch, although you might find females and young cats overlapping.

Quinton pointed to clusters of dots on his maps, depicting GPS groupings, and explained that these indicated where a leopard had made a kill. By visiting these sites, an accurate picture of their diet had been put together. A pie graph showed a menu comprising forty-four percent klipspringer, thirty-four percent dassie and three percent livestock, with the balance made up of a wide range of creatures in very small quantities.

He stressed that his research had proved that farm animals comprised a negligible part of the leopards' diet.

The key to removing them completely from the menu was livestock management. He spoke about his project in Namaqualand, where eco-ranger herders with Anatolian sheep dogs were doing pioneering work with sheep flocks. Employing herders and dogs and placing livestock in pens at night almost entirely eradicated predation. It simply required a mind shift by farmers.

Quinton then showed photographs from his infrared-camera traps. They depicted the wide biodiversity of the mountain, from porcupine and honey badger to caracal and baboon. Next came an image of two frolicking leopard cubs, which had the audience *ahh-ing*. "These little beauties were born on 7 January 2011," said Quinton. "Both have survived and dispersed into the mountains."

When his talk ended, the audience had plenty of questions.

How much did mountain leopards weigh?

Answer: Males were about thirty-five kilograms, which was half that of their cousins elsewhere in Africa.

Were Cape mountain leopards a subspecies in their own right?

Answer: Probably not, although more research had to be done. However, one feature that distinguished them from other leopards was a black rather than a pink nose.

How many Cape leopards were left?

Answer: About thirty adults in the Cederberg and possibly four-hundred in total. It was a terribly fragile population. A bad spate of a disease such as feline Aids could wipe them all out.

Were there any left on Table Mountain or the Cape Peninsula?

Answer: No, although many hikers had reported otherwise.

Quinton would have to be shown photographs to be convinced. The range around Cape Town had shrunk to unsustainable proportions. "You'd find Constantia poodles and Boulders Beach penguins getting nailed if they were still around," said Quinton. "We must assume that peninsula leopards are extinct."

The applause was loud and long. The tour leader stood up to thank Quinton, and told his group that the Cape Leopard Trust survived on donations alone. Would they please give generously. As we were packing up, he came to tell us that a number of guests would be dipping into their purses for the cause. Our trip had not been in vain.

"Fundraising and PR are a huge part of the job," said Quinton as we drove back. "I'd love to be on my own in the mountain, tracking leopards full-time, but it's just not possible anymore. The Trust is a big organisation with staff and responsibilities. We have projects all over the Cape, investors to keep satisfied, and the interested public needs to be informed about our activities."

We returned to Matjiesrivier for supper. Around the barbecue fire, talk was all about the elusive nature of Cape leopards. Quinton had worked at Londolozi for years, where leopards were spotted on almost every game drive. He'd recently visited Phinda Game Reserve in KwaZulu-Natal Province to compare notes with researchers using similar trapping methods. Before they'd even finished setting the last in a series of snares, the first one was triggered by an inquisitive leopard. In the Cederberg, you could wait half a year for that.

"So why on earth do you do it?" I asked.

"Part of the mystery is their elusiveness. I'm not generally a patient man—"

"You can say that again," Elizabeth cut in.

"But I make an exception for leopards. I have to."

Elizabeth told us about the time they had a television crew staying with them for a month, desperate for a sighting. Quinton stared sheepishly into his beer as his wife recounted the incident. Days dragged by and they had no luck. Finally one of the transmitters was triggered at a cage trap high in the mountains. It took them hours to lug the camera equipment to the spot. When they got close enough, the crew set up a shot looking down on the hidden trap. With the cameras rolling, Quinton cautiously approached the cage, only to discover that the cat had managed to escape. At that precise moment, his frustration boiled over, and with a roar of rage, he picked up the cage and hurled it over a cliff, cameras rolling all the while. The TV crew got some lovely footage of an enraged man-leopard.

The next day, Lorraine and Garth had to return to the city to attend their grandchildren's performance in a school concert. Instead of dismantling the three traps and waiting for more volunteers to arrive, I offered to take over the monitoring. This involved checking the frequencies of each trap every couple of hours throughout the day and night. If the pulse doubled from its normal forty beats per minute, a snare had been triggered and I was to summon Quinton pronto. We rigged up an aerial on the roof of my cabin and led the cable through a window so the receiver could reach my bedside table. That way, I wouldn't have to get up in the night to check the signal.

"If the trap is sprung, I'll go in alone and assess the situation," said Quinton. "I don't want you with me at that point. Approaching an angry cat can be terrifying. I was once stalked by a leopard in Londolozi. There's nothing quite like that primal fear."

I imagined a writhing, spitting ball of teeth and claws at the end of a wire, and agreed that it would probably be best if I came later with the vets and their darting rifles. Preferably a hundred metres behind them.

For the rest of my time at Driehoek, I stayed close to the receiver. I took the occasional stroll around the farm or along the lower slopes of Corridor Peak behind the homestead, but felt responsible for the traps. I didn't want a leopard to spend any longer than was necessary with its paw in a noose. However, all frequencies continued to bleat a negative. I set my alarm clock to sound at intervals through the night. Each time I woke to check the receiver, there'd be a thrill of expectation. It was like spinning a roulette wheel: this time I'd be lucky.

Days dragged by, and I began to worry I might sit in that hut for weeks with no reward. Besides, the city had begun to assert itself. First the odd SMS, then phone calls: bills, the plumber, a body-corporate meeting. Eventually, I had no choice but to pack for home.

On my last day in the mountains, Quinton and Elizabeth arrived to take me on a concerted hunt for Spot, the female that frequented our area. It was a final roll of the dice.

Driving up Uilsgat Kloof, we picked up a strong telemetry signal. She was definitely in the valley. But where? Her echo bounced off the rocky walls, making accurate bearings difficult. We parked and got out.

"I'm getting a fairly good signal from the other side of the gorge, halfway up Mied se berg," said Quinton. "You okay for a bit of a hike?"

"Sure," I said unconvincingly. By now, I knew what "a bit of a hike" meant.

As we prepared our packs with water, food, cameras, binoculars and telemetry equipment, Elizabeth happened to glance at the cliff and exclaimed: "Look at those black eagles! They're attacking something!"

"My God, I'll bet you it's Spot," said Quinton, grabbing his binoculars.

We watched the two great birds making an attack run. They approached in a parabolic swoop, then folded their wings and dropped out of the sky in a near-vertical dive. As they plummeted, each bird let out a scream that raised the hairs on the back of my neck. The Stuka dive-bombers of the mountain. At the last moment, when it seemed inevitable they'd smash themselves against the cliff in an explosion of feathers, the birds flared their enormous wings, talons extended, almost brushing the rock as they soared back into the blue.

"There, on that big boulder, she's cowering!" shouted Quinton.

I trained my binoculars in the direction he was pointing, my heart racing. Nothing. Or perhaps a glimpse of movement?

"Where exactly?" I asked.

"The big round rock, above the diagonal one."

I looked again, willing the leopard to show itself. Which round rock, which diagonal one? They were all round or diagonal. There! Had I seen something? Maybe just the hint of cat, a vague feline suggestion? Maybe not.

"She must have slipped behind the rock," said Quinton. "Let's move. Fast. If we angle to the left, we can herd her up the valley towards our traps and maybe get a sighting into the bargain."

"Herding cats," I muttered under my breath as we set off across the valley floor at an unsustainable pace. Quinton and Elizabeth took giraffe strides; mine were more suburban. We came to a stream and my two companions stepped over it without breaking stride. I sloshed through, filling my shoes with mud. By now, every animal in the valley knew about Spot, and the alarm calls of a grey rhebok ahead of us were picked up by a troop of baboons. The valley was a natural amphitheatre, and the sounds echoed around us, backed by a chorus of birdsong. I was thrilled. I felt like David Attenborough in the climactic scene of one of his BBC documentaries.

We scaled the western slope and veered along a contour towards the likely boulder. My two companions had changed from giraffes to klipspringers, their cloven hoofs gripping the rocks as they gambolled ahead. I slipped, grazing a knee. The telemetry, pinging like sonar, told us Spot hadn't moved far, and Quinton motioned us to continue in complete silence.

We came to an outcrop, took off our packs and scrambled up to a ledge. My shoe sent a pebble clip-clopping down the valley. Quinton looked back at me with a frown. Poking our heads over the lip, we scanned the area where Spot should have been. The telemetry told us she was less than fifty metres away, but we just couldn't see her. The dassies on a nearby boulder were going ballistic with their alarm calls. They'd certainly seen her. All we could do was wait for Spot to show herself.

This waiting and staring and telemetrying and looking at each other with quizzical looks went on for about twenty minutes. Then Quinton edged off to the left and we followed, trying not to dislodge any more stones or breathe too loudly.

"She's on the move," whispered Quinton. "You two wait here. I'll try to flush her out."

He clambered down the rock face, angling to the right to force her up the valley into open ground. His telemetry aerial swung back and forth above his head, making him look like Robotman. We scanned the scrub, triangulating our gaze with the direction of Quinton's aerial. How could a big cat vanish into such meagre cover, right under our noses, and wearing a telemetry collar to boot?

After half an hour, Quinton returned, looking dejected. We found some shade and ate our sandwiches.

"As you can see, this is a very, very frustrating game," he said, staring across the valley to where the baboon troop barked lustily, marking Spot's progress somewhere along the opposite slope.

My time was up. I drove out of the enchanted valley, over Uitkyk Pass, and down the winding gravel road to Algeria. My thoughts turned to how, up there in the mountains, the future of leopards was relatively secure. For now, at least. The region had once endured the greatest predator-farmer conflict in the Cape, with up to seventeen leopards killed annually. But in 2007, an area of 1,710 square kilometres had been set aside as the Cederberg Conservancy. With Quinton's help, the entire farming community had agreed to ban gin traps. Livestock farming with sheep, goats and cattle had then been the primary land use; now wine production, olive trees and citrus predominated. Leopards are not vegetarians... and they're teetotallers.

And what of Spot? Had I seen her, or hadn't I? My imagination certainly produced a vision of sorts. Spot was there on the rock, bathed in sunshine, her back arched. She stared up at the great bird falling towards her. Her whiskers bristled as she bared her fangs. Those golden eyes, their pupils narrowed to tiny slits, measured the approach of the eagle, readying herself to strike. A flicking tail, claws anchoring her to the rock, a sinuous body pressed low. I could even hear the soft growl coming from deep inside her, like the sound of distant thunder.

Had I really seen her? Quinton certainly had. Elizabeth might have caught a glimpse. I was less sure. Did the fact that one person in the group achieved a sighting mean that, technically, the group as a whole had seen a leopard? Is one's own pair of flawed, short-sighted eyes that important in the bigger scheme of "the sighting"?

And maybe I had, actually, seen a fleeting shape. A half-sighting or perhaps a "sort of" sighting. Did a half-sighting count as a sighting? If one rounded up the half to a whole, which even the most fastidious accountants permit, then I'd definitely spotted Spot. I *had* seen a Cape mountain leopard! Sort of.

A CROSS BETWEEN A PIG, A RABBIT AND A TOILET BRUSH

Having *almost* bagged a leopard, it was now time to turn my attention to the second impossible animal on my list: the aardvark. I spent the month after returning from the Cederberg planning my next journey. By phoning and emailing a host of conservation bodies and universities, I found out about a dynamic Swedish zoologist, Fredrik Dalerum, who was working in the field of terrestrial animal ecology at Pretoria University. His research covered such mammals as bat-eared foxes, aardwolves and aardvarks.

When I eventually got Fred on the phone, he told me his current studies were primarily on foxes and aardwolves, but there was always a chance of seeing aardvarks if I visited their research site on a farm outside Kimberley in the Northern Cape.

I mentioned that aardwolf had originally been a contender for my Impossible Five. Fred suggested I drop aardvark and switch back to aardwolf. It wasn't a bad idea, especially given how wretchedly elusive aardvarks are. Or perhaps I could embark on my journey with the slightly looser objective of finding an "aard" something, whether it be 'wolf or 'vark, and see which one turned up. However, upon further consideration, I discarded this idea. Aardvarks are the more distinctive, more absurd and more secretive of the two. And I thought they were adorable, more like a made-up creature from a children's book than a living, breathing mammal. Aardvark it would have to be.

One early summer's morning I set off from my flat in Cape Town and drove northeast, through the Huguenot Tunnel, across the lime-green, vineyard-patched Breede River Valley, up the Pass of the Hex and onto the shining plains of the Great Karoo. After a pit-stop KFC lunch in Beaufort West, my route swung north across more Karoo wastes, through sleepy villages shimmering in a siesta haze. Finally, after eleven hours, my Land Rover rumbled into Kimberley, diamond capital of the world.

My home was the Kimberley Club, founded by Cecil John Rhodes in 1881, and styled on Victorian equivalents in London. Stepping from the bright sunshine of a scruffy African street into the cool interiors of the club was somewhat surreal. It's a grand colonial pile whose every detail reminds one of the heady time of the diamond rush, when Kimberley was a financial centre of the British Empire. Rhodes was still unnervingly present in statues, busts, photographs and paintings. The great imperialist appeared to be watching my every move.

I was led to my room up a creaky flight of stairs.

There were dark panelled walls, stained-glass windows and the drone of wooden ceiling fans. Pictures in the corridors were dedicated to the Anglo-Boer War siege of Kimberley, when the town was surrounded by Boer forces and the British dug in for a long defence at the turn of the last century. Rhodes found himself trapped there, and directed many of the operations from his table in the club's dining room. Photographs showed British artillery, trenches, parades and the damage caused by Boer shelling. Some depicted soldiers in cricket-eleven poses, bent on giving the away team, camped outside town, a good thrashing. The whole affair seems to have had the air of a Boy Scout adventure for jingoistic imperialists, providing the chance to snatch a spot of glory for king and country.

Wandering the rooms offered a window on a long-forgotten Cape. Here was a jockey chair presented to the club by Winston Churchill's father, there a piece of shrapnel retrieved from a gentleman's leg during the shelling. Outside my bedroom was a Gatling gun and a row of artillery shells, produced in Rhodes's foundry for the Long Cecil cannon, with the words "compliments of CJR" engraved on each.

I'd just begun to unpack my bags and was envisioning a shower, quiet supper and early night after the long drive, when my cell-phone rang. Fred was heading into the field that evening—did I want to join him? Could I be ready in forty-five minutes?

I grabbed a shower and trotted downstairs for a quick bite. It was only me and a timid Chinese tourist in the dining room. I hadn't realised that "quick" is not easy in the Kimberley Club, with its genteel air and a stooped, snail-like waiter of the old school. The room echoed to the sound of a tinkling piano, chandeliers were dimmed and there I regally sat in the old imperialist's corner chair, twiddling my thumbs. A lonely fly droned above me, tracing an uneven halo around my head. The Karoo lamb took forever to arrive. I gulped it down with undignified haste, skipped pudding and emerged from the building to find Fred leaning against his Tata pick-up truck.

"Fantastic Mister Fox, the Impossible Five hunter! Hop in," he said.

"Dr Dalerum, I presume." We shook hands.

Fred, a short, muscular fellow with unkempt hair, a scruffy beard-in-progress and looking like a pocket Viking, was barefoot, and dressed in tattered shorts and a checked shirt. I noticed that he had jottings and scientific equations written in ballpoint pen on his legs. He'd apparently run out of paper on his last game drive. I'd brought along a warm jacket and woolly hat, anticipating a cold desert night. Fred's Scandinavian blood would obviously keep him warm. In fact, he confided that he'd been a competitive cross-country skier, which explained his muscular physique.

Driving out to the farm, Fred talked about the various projects he had on the go. In his capacity as research fellow at the Mammal Research Institute of Pretoria University, he was supervising eight postgraduate students, most of them conducting their studies in the field outside Kimberley.

Benfontein is a game farm owned by the De Beers mining group. It has been made available to students for a host of research initiatives, including work on ant-eating chats, termites and black-footed cats. It's a ten-kilometre by ten-kilometre piece of feral land situated ten kilometres southeast of Kimberley. We drew up beside a homestead where most of the students resided, and transferred from Fred's Tata to the department's research vehicle: a green, 1972 Land Rover. The Landie was, to put it politely, utilitarian. It was not so much a vehicle as the idea of a vehicle. Anything that wasn't absolutely essential to propulsion had long since been eaten away or rattled off.

We lumbered down a farm track under a coagulation of stars, scrub hares bounding through the veld ahead of us. The open vehicle sucked in its own diesel fumes and dust like a vacuum cleaner, and soon we were coughing and choking. The night was cold and I pulled on my jacket and woolly cap. Fred looked bemused.

"Our work here is primarily on aardwolves and bat-eared foxes," he said in a clipped Swedish accent. "We haven't got stuck into aardvarks yet. They're terribly shy. In the beginning, we looked at many possible sites for our research. I discounted national parks (too much bureaucracy) and popular parks (too many tourists getting in the way) and Big Five areas (I didn't want to be eaten while monitoring on foot). We settled on Benfontein because it's flat, easy, open terrain and it's favoured by all three animals."

"What sort of research are you doing on aardwolves?" I asked.

"At the moment we're evaluating five different enzyme immunoassays for the non-invasive analysis of reproductive and adrenocortical steroid hormone metabolites."

"Um, can you say that again?"

"At the moment we're evaluating—"

"Never mind."

"Basically, I spend a lot of time looking at aardwolf faeces. We've taken hundreds of scat samples. We dry them, sift them, put them through strainers, wash them and then analyse the contents."

"Yes, I've just been with Quinton Martins in the Cederberg. Same thing. Another lunatic. Rather you than me. But it's really aard*varks* I'm after, not wolves."

"We don't have any collared yet, although there's always a chance. They're around, they're just very hard to spot."

It didn't sound promising.

"Why don't you switch to aardwolf?" he suggested once again.

"I've kind of got my heart set on aardvark."

"Have you got something against aardwolves? They're fantastic animals."

"No, no, it's just that—"

"Aardwolves have one of the most specialised diets of all carnivores. More than aardvarks. They only—"

"But Fred, I really, really want to find an aardvark."

"Humph," he said.

That night, even the collared aardwolves were proving elusive, so we latched onto a pair of foraging bat-eared foxes. We trailed them for an hour, Fred tracking their movements on his GPS and scrawling notes on his thigh while I tried to take photographs as they danced through the beam of our spotlight. They were a lively pair with sleek grey bodies and enormous black ears. It was certainly no hardship postponing the hunt for one or other "aard" until another night, and spending time with these lovelies instead.

Next morning, after an imperial-sized full English breakfast, I drove to the McGregor Museum where Fred was renting rooms and a laboratory. The rambling Victorian building had been the town's sanatorium (built as a "recuperative hotel" in 1897), and had served as Cecil Rhodes's headquarters during the siege. A receptionist led me through vast rooms, many of them dedicated to the siege, then up a flight of stairs to the attic where Fred and Charmaine Theron, one of his entomology MSc students, were eating their rather more frugal breakfast. Frankly, it looked like aardwolf scat in a bowl of milk. Their accommodation had the air of typical student digs: piles of unwashed crockery, thundering rock music, unmade beds, clothes on the floor and pyramids of scientific bric-a-brac cluttering every corner.

I joined them at the kitchen table. The dragon tattoo that snaked up Charmaine's arm belied a shy demeanour, and it took some coaxing to get her to explain her area of expertise. It turned out she was researching termites—in particular, termite predation by animals such as aardvarks and aardwolves. If Fred couldn't find me an aardvark, maybe Charmaine's termites could lead me to one.

Fred disappeared to run errands, and Charmaine took

me down to the lab to show me her research. The room was a chaotic jumble of paraphernalia left behind by dozens of scientists, along with the detritus of countless experiments. There were nets, stacks of journals, spotlights, tripods and rows of jars filled with insects floating in ethanol. The floor was covered with plastic boxes, each containing samples from different termite mounds. Charmaine was investigating how termites interacted and defended their territory. I found a bar stool and watched as she extracted an earthy sample swarming with soldier termites and placed it in a Tupperware dish beneath a video camera. Using a small paint brush, she caught hold of a single termite from a different mound and measured it with a calliper. A blob of yellow paint was painstakingly applied to its head using a paper clip.

"Why don't you just spray-paint the critter?" I joked.

"Actually, we tried that," she said, "but we killed dozens."

"Even as a non-scientist, I might have guessed that," I said.

"Mmm," said Charmaine as she transferred the termite to its new home. She switched on the camera as the yellow-headed creature was deposited into a Coliseum of hostile termites. It was immediately attacked and sprayed with a sticky, defensive secretion containing toxic terpenes, hosed through a nozzle on the defenders' heads. After a few minutes of struggle, the invader rolled onto its back, legs in the sky, very dead. Charmaine found another victim, from a different mound, and repeated the process.

Exciting as it all was—initially, at least—I had issues with her methodology. Maybe these termites had an aversion to other termites wearing big blond wigs? Maybe they didn't like the smell of paint? I tried to imagine an alien with a mop of Dulux yellow hair landing uninvited in my living room, deposited by a giant, airborne paintbrush. I'd also probably spray the creature with whatever insect repellent came to hand. There were countless other variables, but I held my tongue.

"I'm comparing the reactions I get to termites from a mound that's ten metres away to one that's fifty or a hundred metres away," she said. "In effect, I'm mapping the spatial extent of a colony by looking at behaviour. You see, we don't think that one mound equals one colony. We find that some intruders are left completely in peace. Then again, a termite from an adjacent mound sometimes gets the most violent reaction. We're still working on it."

"So basically you spend all day, every day, making termite snuff movies," I said.

"Yup, pretty much."

"You should think about YouTube. Or perhaps a limited cinema release."

"Mmm." She wasn't listening.

Next, Charmaine showed me how she simulated rain by spraying the mound samples with water to see how this affected behaviour. She explained that rain meant more above-ground activity, and hence increased predation by mammals. When it comes to predators, aardvarks are the main enemy, as they have claws powerful enough to break open a mound. Termites use their standard method of defence: spraying the intruder with terpenes. After a while, this takes effect as the ingestion of too many terpenes can cause liver damage (which is why the missus always grumbles when Porky spends too much time down at the Termite and Mound). The aardvark either retreats or tries to dig deeper to escape the soldiers' spray, and get at the defenceless workers below. Charmaine told me she had two-hundred termite mounds marked, and was studying which ones were chosen by aardvarks, and from which side the mammals preferred to mount their attack.

"Have you ever seen an aardvark on Benfontein?" I asked.

"Nope. I've seen their holes a million times, though."

Great, I thought. My chances were not looking good. Perhaps I should change to aardwolves after all. I watched a few hours of *Termite Wars* before Fred came to pick me up. We returned to the farm and prepared for the evening's hunt. Fred intended to dart one of the aardwolves whose telemetry collar was about to run out of battery power. And we could "look for some aardvarks at the same time".

By day, I got a better sense of Benfontein. The farm occupied an amphitheatre-shaped watershed that had once been an ancient lake and was now gently sloping grassland. "Over the millennia, abundant water and good grazing attracted not only wildlife," said Fred. "Wherever you walk on the farm, you find Stone Age tools."

For a few hours, we drove this way and that, bumping

over rocky ground. The cloud-free sky was a dark-blue canopy and brittle yellow grass stretched to the horizon. It was debilitatingly hot. Every so often, Fred would stop and use his telemetry antenna to check the location of various animals. At one point, the signal grew very strong. We got out and walked to an abandoned aardvark hole.

"As you can hear from the transmitter, the aardwolf is using this as a sleeping den. He's definitely down there. We'll return at sunset and wait for him to emerge."

Driving back to Kimberley, Fred spoke of matters close to his heart: conservation, the depletion of natural resources and how the world needed to change. He envisioned a new form of socialism that was the opposite of contemporary growth models. Most farmers were only getting about ten percent yield from their land. Farming needed to be much more labour-intensive, which was not great economically, but made sense for the planet. He felt that conservation was, in a way, a red herring. "The focus of change should be people's minds."

Fred also talked about the other branches of his mammal research. One project looked at how animals responded when a predator was reintroduced into an area where it had become extinct. "A large component of the ecological effect of predation does not lie in the actual killing of prey, but in the anti-predator responses of the prey," he explained. "They shift habitats, start to forage different patches, grow skittish and so on. I'm interested in seeing how rapidly animals lose predator recognition, and then how quickly they regain it when predators return.

"We've been working in one reserve where lions are extinct, and another where they are being reintroduced. I start with sound recognition. I've rigged a big loudspeaker on the back of my Tata, and drive around the reserve playing recordings of lions, wolves—which are an unknown predator in Africa—and Celine Dion."

"An unknowable predator?" I said.

"Not exactly; we use her because she represents a strange noise that has nothing to do with predation."

"That's what you think. I'm trying to picture how I'd respond if I were an impala, minding my own business having a quiet graze, and heard Celine Dion coming through the long grass singing 'The Power of Love'. I think every instinct in my body would scream 'run for your life'."

"That was my thought too, but in fact they're more scared of lions."

"I find that hard to believe."

"It's the honest-to-God truth. I was as surprised as you. We've actually been thinking of trying a whole range of music types, heavy metal, jazz, even classical."

"Please tell me you'll spare them Boney M."

That evening, Charmaine, Fred and I met at Halfway House Pub for an early pizza dinner. Conversation turned to the procedure, should we manage to dart an aardwolf. It was similar to Quinton's modus operandi with leopards. The collar would be changed, while blood and hair samples would be taken. The latter is good for DNA, and its stable isotopes yield a decent diet analysis. Fred would also measure and weigh the aardwolf and assess the wear on its teeth to try and determine age.

"If we see an aardvark, can we dart it instead?" I asked.

"No," said Fred. Between mouthfuls of pizza, he talked about his many years of study. He'd done his PhD on wolverines, and spent most of the time on a frozen lake in Alaska where the temperature reached minus 45°C. He'd got up to a lot of other hair-brained exploits during his career. Like giving CPR to meerkat pups, or assessing the diet of Arctic foxes when lemming numbers were low, or studying male-biased sex ratios among human billionaires, or helping an ex-girlfriend fit transmitters to sheep on an island in Scotland. In the latter instance, glue didn't work on the oily wool, so they tried chewing gum, which worked perfectly. They conducted an exhaustive experiment on different brands of gum to see which was the stickiest after mastication. He admitted that it was sometimes best not to let funders know exactly how their money was being spent.

Benfontein had its own crop of interesting experiments on the go. For instance, one scientist was collecting semen samples from black-footed cats.

"But *how*?" I asked, a parade of inappropriate images hotfooting it through my head.

"Electro-ejaculation," said Fred.

"Ah," I said, nodding appreciatively.

"You know, sticking a probe up the cat's anus to stimulate the prostrate and make it ejaculate."

"Not very romantic," I said.

"That depends," said Fred. "We did it to ground squirrels a few years back."

"Fun?"

59

"Not as much fun as doing it to an elephant."

"Of course," I said.

After supper, we loaded up the vehicle in the parking lot of the museum. There was a dart gun with its accoutrements, telemetry equipment and hot-water bottles. Charmaine explained that these were not for us, but rather for the aardwolf. Once darted, their thermoregulation apparently gets disabled by the drug. On a hot day, they can overheat, and on an icy night, they can die of cold if the scientists don't artificially regulate their temperature.

"Why don't we put tea in the one hot-water bottle and coffee in the other?" I suggested.

"No," said Charmaine.

We reached Benfontein just after sunset and transferred once again to the Jurassic Land Rover. Charmaine stood in the back, Ben-Hur style, a powerful spotlight in her hand. I sat in the passenger seat, entrusted with the dart gun. We drove out to the burrow Fred had located that afternoon, only to find the aardwolf had already vacated his residence for a night of foraging.

Fred was not amused. This was the tenth night he'd tried to dart this particular animal, and he was losing patience. We drove a few grids, then picked up a telemetry signal to the north and headed off-road. After twenty minutes of uncomfortable driving, Charmaine cried, "There he is!"

Her spotlight picked out a faint shape at the very extremity of its range. Fred floored the pedal and we thumped along, bouncing over boulders and into aardvark holes, Charmaine hanging on for dear life in the back. The aardwolf was not particularly disturbed by our presence, but wouldn't stay still for a moment. He hopped back and forth, halting only to leave the briefest scent marking, before setting off again. "As you can see, he's a pathological urinater," said Fred. "Aardwolves have made territorial marking an obsession."

On and on the animal bounded, and on and on we bounced.

"Does he never stop?" I pleaded after half an hour of this punishment.

"Only to forage on termites," said Charmaine. "And then only for a few seconds."

At times, he ran across open ground and following him was relatively easy. At others, he'd disappear into the long grass, and keeping up became hard work. Charmaine swept the veld with her spotlight, trying to catch sight of a bobbing head that looked like a seal duck-diving through waves of grass. Often we'd lose him, and Fred would resort to telemetry again.

The night progressed in this manner. It was, it must be said, a lovely night, with the stars twinkling gaily above and the lights of Kimberley twinkling gaily on the horizon, but frustration levels were rising. The vehicle was not in any way comfortable. The seats had long since unsprung themselves, and the doors fallen off. The dart gun bounced in my lap, and I had to be careful not to poke Charmaine in the stomach with the muzzle.

The aardwolf meanwhile seemed high on cocaine, manically ferreting and snuffing this way and that.

In my head, our chase began to assume epic proportions, like a metaphor for aspiration, or futility. In his own sweet way, the aardwolf was growing into the very symbol of my quest. Elusive, ever-receding, increasingly infuriating. In short, *im-bloody-possible*.

Finally, the animal discovered a large nest of termites and settled down for a proper forage. Fred stopped and checked the range through his scope. With this particular dart gun (given the low pressure used for the projectile so as not to hurt the animal), you had to get within twelve metres of the target. Fred flicked on his head torch, opened a case and took out a cylindrical dart with a red tail. He carefully squeezed a combination of sedative and anaesthetic from a syringe into the projectile, then loaded the gun.

While he was doing this, I had a chance to study the creature through binoculars. It looked like a small, striped hyena with a dark snout and large pinkish ears. The tawny body was shaggy: a diminutive Alsatian dog, I thought. "He's helluva pretty, hey?" whispered Charmaine in my ear. "He doesn't have powerful enough claws to break open a mound. So he's got to make do with mopping up after an aardvark raid or catching termites out in the open. Aardvarks switch to ants in summer, but aardwolves eat only termites. This guy can guzzle up to 300,000 of them a night."

As Fred took aim, the aardwolf looked up. There was a flash of orange eyes, and off he bounded. I was hastily handed the gun (taking care to keep my finger away from the trigger), and we resumed the chase. On and on and on he ran.

Eventually, mercifully, the wretched creature stopped for a more substantial toilet break of the number-two variety. This was our chance. Fred let the vehicle roll to a stop and checked the range: twelve metres exactly. "A bloke can't even take a dump in peace around here," muttered Charmaine in the back.

I handed over the gun. The aardwolf was still squatting, a far-away expression on his face. Fred raised himself in the seat and took aim through the telescopic sights. Interminable seconds ticked by as the hunter made sure of his aim. I watched his trigger finger. The aardwolf glanced up and made to move. Fred squeezed. A metallic snap. The dart was so slow you could easily track its cumbersome, silver-and-red arc. It hit the ground with a puff of dust one metre short. The aardwolf leapt into the air as though he'd been stung and catapulted into the long grass.

"Damn this gun!" yelled Fred as he started the engine, and slammed the vehicle into gear. We were off again. The rifle was an old one he'd borrowed, and had been malfunctioning of late. "Every now and then it has an uneven pressure release," he grumbled. "Bloody useless thing."

Now the animal was running with more purpose, and we had to travel at greater speeds to keep up. Wheels bounced through aardvark holes, Charmaine held on with whitened knuckles, the spotlight stabbed wildly at the dark. Our quarry ducked through a fence and forced us into a long detour to find a gate. I leapt out to open it while Charmaine swung the telemetry. "That way!"

We were on his tail again. Bump, bump, bump and still his energy never flagged. This continued for another half hour until we noticed that the spotlight's beam had begun to fade. Seeing as it ran off the car battery, this was a problem. We gave up the chase and came to a halt.

Fortunately, there was a spare battery. Charmaine and I stretched our legs while Fred got down to repairs. Half his body disappeared beneath the bonnet and the occasional curse was heard from within. It looked as though he was being devoured by a portly green hippo. Eventually the second battery was fitted, but we decided to call it a night and drove back to the farmhouse across the wide, ancient veld where dinosaur had once fought dinosaur, Stone Age man had hunted antelope, Boer had scrapped with Brit, and Fred had gotten mightily frustrated.

"I have to be as much a mechanic as a scientist on these damn projects," groused Fred. "We have a bunch of old cars and our students hammer them. They drive into trees, put oil in the radiators, snap the axels in aardvark holes... and then they phone me in Pretoria and ask what they should do!"

My chances of finding an aardvark with Fred and Charmaine were looking remote, so I decided to switch to my next option, a game reserve in the Kalahari Desert. I went to say goodbye to the two scientists at the museum.

"You're absolutely sure you don't want to stick around?" asked Fred. "We could try another darting session tonight."

"As wonderful as aardwolves are—and they are indeed, Fred—I really need to find an aardvark."

"Oh all right then." He shook my hand. I gave Charmaine a hug and climbed into my car.

"Let us know how you get on," she said. I pulled away.

"What have you got against aardwolves?!" shouted Fred, grinning.

"Nothing! Nothing at all!" I called as I turned into Egerton Road and headed out of town.

My destination was the luxurious Tswalu Game Reserve, reputedly one of the best places in southern Africa to see aardvark, especially in winter, when they emerged during daylight hours. It was already early summer, but I was hoping for better luck than I'd had in Kimberley. Driving north to Kuruman, the landscape grew ever drier and more sparsely vegetated. After three hours, I passed the appropriately named Hotazel, a village living up to its sizzling name, with my vehicle's thermometer nudging forty. The road ahead dissolved into a blurry mirage as I sped deeper into the desert.

A left turn off the R31 took me down a long gravel road through terrain dotted with camelthorn and blackthorn trees to the reserve's main gate. Tswalu is owned by the Oppenheimer family. At more than one-thousand square kilometres and comprising forty-six former farms, it is by far the largest piece of privately owned land in South Africa. The farms have all been restored to their former, wild state: "tswalu" means "new beginning" in Tswana. Due to the wide diversity of habitats, ranging from quartzite mountains to savannah, the reserve is home to more than two-hundred-and-forty species of birds and eighty mammal species. But I was only interested in seeing one.

I was met by staff at the gate and escorted to Motse, Tswalu's main lodge. Set on the western slopes of the Korannaberg, it has a large thatched reception area with decks and two swimming pools. The interiors are all done in earth colours, with big chairs carved from tree trunks, ochre-coloured sofas, wicker armchairs, suspended basket fish-traps and an enormous fireplace. Outside there's dry-stone walling, a shaded dining area and private sun decks. A solar-heated pond lies in a rockery at the base of a small waterfall, and is set at eye level with a nearby waterhole, so guests can watch animals drinking while immersed. It was all terribly posh.

There are four chalets on either side of the lodge, each individually styled in impeccable bush taste. Mine had a gigantic bed draped with mosquito netting, and a fireplace flanked by log piles for winter nights. A study area fronted by a glass wall offered gorgeous views of the veld, a place I could happily spend the heat of the day writing. Thankfully, there was air-conditioning.

At teatime that afternoon, I met my guide Jolyon Neytzell-de-Wilde to discuss the coming days' aardvark hunt. Jolyon was a rugged man of the bush with a powerful physique, short-cropped hair and stubbly beard. He came across as the gruff, no-nonsense type, but every now and then he burst into an infectious laugh that started and ended with a delightful snort.

We stood before a mural map of Tswalu, and he pointed out the areas where we'd be concentrating our search. Aardvarks only emerge after dark, so our first game drive would be a pleasant evening's orientation followed by a dune dinner with the other guests, after which we'd knuckle down to the hunt proper.

Getting into the open 4X4, we were joined by William Gatsene, a Tswana who grew up on a nearby farm and is considered one of the finest trackers in the Kalahari. It was clear from his high cheekbones, prematurely wrinkled face and yellow-tinged skin, that the blood of the San people, Bushman hunter gatherers, ran freely in his veins. William climbed into the jockey seat on the front of the bonnet, which offered an uninterrupted view of the veld. From this position, he could scan the sand roads for spoor.

"William is absolutely bloody amazing," said Jolyon under his breath as we pulled away. "A few weeks ago he spotted a lion sleeping in long grass seven-hundred metres away. No-one else could see it, not even with binoculars. If anyone's gonna get you an aardvark, it's William."

"And a pangolin, while we're at it?" I suggested, jumping ahead to the next animal on my list.

"Well, now, we'll have to think long and hard about that little guy," he said. "But let's not get ahead of ourselves. First things first."

We drove off into an arid landscape of pale grasslands and red sand dunes. The breeze came in gusts of hot, desert breath. Animal sightings were easy and regular: eland, tsessebe, red hartebeest, wildebeest and pale giraffes that looked as though they'd been dipped in bleach. Big birds too: kori bustard, black-chested snake eagle, secretary bird. I thought of how my childhood sightings list would have been filling up.

Jolyon talked about his passion for the Kalahari. He loved its extremes, its unpredictability, and was fascinated by the way plants and animals adapted to the harsh conditions. Gemsbok had cricket-bat-shaped hairs to reflect heat and avoid losing moisture; some scorpions could dig holes twenty metres deep; springboks had specialised loops of Henle that extracted water from waste passing through their kidneys; and some plants actually retreated underground during dry spells. Below the surface and away from the sun's rays, it's much cooler, which is one reason why many desert creatures, especially aardvarks and pangolins, spend so much time underground.

The sun began to settle on the horizon as we made our way to a scarlet dune decorated with hurricane lanterns. The Tswalu staff had created an encampment for a bush barbecue under the stars. It was a makeshift caravanserai with a line of Land Rovers drawn up on the slope of the dune, flares and fires lit, kelims and throw cushions arranged on the sand, and camp chairs facing the peachy dusk. Venus glowed uncannily bright in the west, and a flirty Mercury joined her, glittering with almost as much lustre. The wind had died and the day's heat simmered down to a pleasant balminess. The smell of meat on the fire drifted across camp as guests gathered around an ad hoc bar to recount the events of their game drives. One group had spent their time watching the antics at a meerkat manor, another had followed a lion pride on the hunt, while the French party had tracked a black rhino.

Dinner was served in a dune hollow, and went the

whole hog—starched tablecloths and the finest silver. After a leisurely meal of jerky salad, kudu steak and milk tart, Jolyon, William and I headed back out on the trail, now earnestly in search of aardvarks. We drove west into wild country. The rest of the guests made for home, and we watched their headlights and spotlights moving like strange insects across the plain back to the lodge. Within half an hour, ours was perhaps the only vehicle out and about in a thousand square kilometres of wilderness.

We crisscrossed a promising section of the reserve, William playing his beam back and forth over the veld. The air was filled with the sound of barking geckos. A host of fiery eyes stared back at us from the blackness. Spring hares bounded over the dunes like Kalahari kangaroos, and a herd of gemsbok tracked our progress with their rapier heads.

"Cape fox," said William, holding up a hand.

Jolyon took his foot off the accelerator and let us glide to a stop. The creature snuffled in the grass thirty metres to our right. I was delighted. Cape fox had been an impossible-five contender, and is one of southern Africa's most elusive nocturnal animals. I gazed at the pale little predator, almost white in the glow of the spotlight. It had a sweet pointy nose, big ears, a lean body and a bushy oversized tail. It hopped about in the long grass, pouncing on insectivorous morsels.

The drive yielded other pleasures, such as a lesser spotted genet slinking into the darkness at the limit of William's beam. At one point, Jolyon applied the brakes without warning and stepped down from the vehicle (there was no driver's door on this Land Rover). He crouched and made a grab, coming up with a barking gecko between his fingers. The tiny creature had big eyes, a reddish body and pink limbs. Despite their size, they can produce a considerable din on a quiet desert night.

So much for foxes, genets and geckos: I needed an aardvark. It was getting late, however, and Jolyon decided to abandon the hunt and try again just before dawn. Approaching the Korannaberg, we drove into a wall of earthy heat. The west-facing slope, roasted by the afternoon sun, had retained its warmth like a giant baked potato.

I climbed into bed and lay under my diaphanous mosquito net, unable to sleep. Somewhere, a Cape eagle owl hooted; a jackal emitted a shrill, strangled cry. The crickets maintained their insistent calling, which echoed and eddied across the desert sands. It seemed I'd hardly closed my eyes when the alarm clock sounded. It was 4am and time to get on the road again. The sky was still as black as a panther outside.

I joined William and Jolyon on the vehicle as a vague rosiness began to stain the east. The air's chill would not last long. We drove out of camp past a line of upturned bins: the honey badgers had been making a nuisance of themselves again in the night. All around us, the veld was waking up. A line of gemsboks plodded towards a waterhole, kicking up clouds of dust. Springboks danced across our path, prancing in acrobatic bounds. The rim of the Korannaberg turned to honey as the sun's first ray arced overhead.

We stopped on the crest of a dune for coffee. Jolyon laid a cloth on the bonnet with rusks and biscuits. The crimson-breasted shrike watching us from an acacia branch looked as though it had been pricked by the thorns that surrounded it. An eastern clapper lark soared into the air, emitting a staccato slapping noise, then plummeted to the earth with a kamikaze-like "foowee" sound. Not for our benefit, or just for a lark, but rather to impress the lady larks, or so William assured me.

Jolyon directed my gaze to the ground. "The *Kalahari Times*, read all about it," he said. Looking more closely, I noticed that the sand was crisscrossed with spoor of every shape and size. Jolyon pointed out how it was easiest to read when the sun was low, throwing longer shadows. He showed me the tracks of insects, birds and mice, and was able to tell how long they had been there by looking at how much the edges had eroded and whether there was fresh spoor on top of them. It was like learning another alphabet.

"Check this out," he said, picking up a piece of dried faeces. "Aardvark. You can see by all the unchewed grass in the dung."

We followed the tracks to an extensive burrow system, metres deep and comprising many chambers and several entrances. The aardvark's prodigious claws make it Africa's most powerful digger, and its mining and engineering capabilities are legendary. "I think this bloke's vacated," said Jolyon, sticking his head down a hole.

"Aard-house?" I offered.

"Very underground," he said.

"Dark?"

"Ja, terribly *noir*." Jolyon was sharp as a porcupine quill.

We continued searching for fresh spoor until the sun got too high for tracking. Back in camp, I spent a lazy day beside the pool watching the antics of nesting masked weaver birds, swallows drinking on the wing and white butterflies swirling like confetti. A kudu with Medusa horns stooped to drink from the waterhole, watching me closely in case I made a threatening move. A warthog bustled past, tail in the air, running an important errand. I lay on my lounger feeling completely at peace, embraced by a dome of cobalt sky and the muscular arms of the Korannaberg.

When it grew too hot beside the pool, I retreated to my room and snoozed in the jaws of a predatory sofa. At some point in the blurry afternoon, I woke to find a female nyala seeking coolness in the shadow of my chalet. She looked at me indifferently, then sat down under a thorn tree. I didn't move a muscle. After a while she was joined by a foal which also paid me no attention, plonking down next to her mother. I'd been told that the previous owners of Tswalu had kept nyalas, an antelope not associated with desert, and that they had taken to hanging about the lodge.

As the buck were partially habituated, I stood up cautiously and approached them. They chewed the cud unconcerned. I sat on the ground a few metres from the pair. The mother got up and approached me tentatively. I held out a hand and she sniffed, dark wet nostrils flaring at the unfamiliar scent. She took a step nearer and nuzzled her head against my shoulder. A stubby horn snagged my shirt. I was thrilled.

The foal came to take a closer look. I remained seated, which meant their heads were at my eye level. The baby gave a perfunctory sniff and lay down beside me. By now, more nyalas had arrived to seek the shade of the thorn trees around the chalet, and I found myself inside a herd. A twitching nose, a sigh, the lethargic flap of an ear, a hoof scratch, and ever the singing heat. It appeared they'd forgotten that in their midst sat the most lethal predator of all: Man. Having become a temporary member of the herd, I was able to take photographs, sketch and write notes for a most companionable hour.

That night, we set off hunting aardvark once more. Conversation on the vehicle ranged widely, seemingly stretched by the Kalahari's broad horizons. Desert life, friends and family, bush lore, close escapes and the silly questions asked by foreign guests. "'Do giraffes eat meat?' asks this one chap," said Jolyon. "'Why doesn't the lodge mow the grass so we can see the animals better?' And another: 'Do zebras hunt in packs?'"

Jolyon also talked about that other impossible species: women. He had fathered a son with a previous partner. "No regrets, but the bushveld won in the end. Nowadays there's the occasional girlfriend, but my job is eight weeks on, two weeks off, which doesn't go down too well with the ladyfolk. Ja man, despite being constantly among guests, it's a solitary life, if you know what I mean."

He'd been doing the job for twelve years, which is

a long innings for a guide. Most burn out after a few years and move to managerial positions or back to the city. Jolyon enjoyed a challenge like the aardvark one I'd posed, as it relieved him of the daily Big Five round demanded by most guests. Talk turned to our chosen animal. I learnt that due to their wide habitat tolerance, aardvarks are distributed throughout Africa, but nowhere are they common. These secretive, solitary creatures are predominantly nocturnal, but can be crepuscular in the Kalahari winter, being seen fairly regularly at dawn and dusk. Scientists regard the aardvark as a key species in the eco-system, as they're important predators of colonial insects (those that live in colonies, not the empire-building kind), and make a significant, if indirect, contribution by creating homes for many other creatures through their industrious burrowing.

Jolyon spoke about the aardvarks he'd encountered during his career. "We see them quite often here in the Kalahari. They're such ridiculous creatures, hey. It's amazing that evolution hasn't bred them out of existence by now. In lion-rich areas, their numbers are often low. They regularly get killed by cats but not eaten, perhaps 'cause they don't taste so nice. I've often seen females with heavy claw marks down their backs, but I think this is more the result of males trying to mount them than lions."

"Randy male lions?"

"Nah, aardvark chicks aren't pretty enough."

It was nearly midnight and our drive was proving uneventful again. With rotten luck in the Cederberg and

Kimberley, I was beginning to register an undercurrent of grumpiness, fatalism even. Maybe my five chosen animals really were impossible.

Suddenly, William's beam picked out two large bunny ears poking above the grass forty metres to our right. A gap in the vegetation revealed an oversized version of Alice's white rabbit.

"Aardvark," hissed Jolyon, switching off the engine and letting the vehicle coast to a halt. The crickets took over.

This was it: my first impossible! I was so surprised I didn't know quite what to feel. An aardvark, in the flesh. My heart boomed like a bass drum. My hands were shaking so much I couldn't take a photograph.

Without saying a word, Jolyon and I climbed off the left-hand side of the vehicle while William kept his beam trained on the ears. Jolyon was carrying a powerful torch with a red filter, which disturbs animals less than a bright, white light.

"Don't let the grass brush your legs," he whispered. "Move between the clumps."

We edged forward. I found myself trying not to breathe. Excitement had caught up and overtaken my initial surprise. The creature was out in the open, snuffling at the ground for termites. When we got within twenty-five metres, Jolyon switched on his torch. The aardvark lifted its head and stared straight at us, small eyes glowing red in the light. It looked like a termite mound on legs, a bush Eeyore. Hunched stance, piggy-like body, enormous ears and a ridiculously long, nozzle-like snout. I was instantly, head-over-heels in love with one of the most endearing animals I'd ever seen. Not exactly handsome, but its quirkiness was its charm.

"Mixture between a pig, a rabbit and a toilet brush," muttered Jolyon. I would have none of it. To me, this was beauty incarnate, albeit a connoisseur's kind of beauty.

We strayed too close and the aardvark grew wary, moving off with a shuffling gait like an old man in a trench coat. We followed, but the animal was deceptively fast, and there was no way we could keep up. Soon a pair of long white ears slipped into the tall grass and was gone.

Back on the vehicle, I felt like a million dollars. I'd had my first, proper, incontestable sighting of a member of the Impossible Five. My quest was back on track, and all was well.

THE WALKING ARTICHOKE

There were still a few days left at Tswalu before I was due at my next destination, a game ranch where I was to hunt for the utterly impossible pangolin. The plan was to join a young zoologist doing research for his master's. He had attached transmitters to a few of these creatures, and was tracking them on a nightly basis. But the real prize would be to find one for myself in the wild without the help of telemetry. So I set Jolyon the task of bagging a pangolin. Needless to say, the expression on his face suggested he'd accidentally swallowed a shongololo. Top-end safari lodges such as Tswalu pride themselves on catering to a guest's every need, no matter how outlandish or demanding. And I needed a pangolin.

"As a matter of fact, Tswalu is probably the best place in South Africa to find one," said Jolyon. "However, before you get your hopes up, be aware that I've only seen five in all the years I've worked here."

Five is a lot more than most field guides see in a lifetime. Jolyon and William agreed to give it a concerted and single-minded bash. The rest of my stay would be focused exclusively on finding a pangolin.

Southern African ground pangolins (*Smutsia temminckii*) are strange, prehistoric-looking creatures. Their bodies are covered in an armour of heavy brown scales, making them appear more dinosaur than mammal. The scales are made of fused hair, similar to rhino horn or human fingernails. They walk on their hind legs, using their tails for balance. The head is tiny and the muzzle tapers to a point with smaller scales along the snout. Adult males can reach a length of more than a metre and weigh up to eighteen kilograms.

They are secretive animals that spend up to twenty hours a day underground, usually in abandoned aardvark burrows. Their long, curved front claws are sharp and used to open ant nests during feeding. Pangolins have no teeth, but in their place are narrow raised ridges of bone. Their insect prey is swallowed directly into the muscular stomach, where it's ground up with the help of grit and sand simultaneously ingested. Pangolins are solitary foragers and predominantly nocturnal. They are perfectly adapted to their environment and have been around for forty million years, which puts the 0,2 million of *Homo sapiens* nicely into perspective.

The southern African ground pangolin is one of a family of nine. It has cousins in China, India and Malaysia, as well as two small tree-climbing relatives and a big brother—the giant pangolin—in Africa. Ground pangolins are sparsely distributed in regions that abound with ants and termites across southern Africa and up into

East Africa as far as Sudan.

The following morning, we set off into a dawn filled with purple clouds, searching for pangolin tracks. William watched the road and surrounding dunes, his eyes scanning like radar. He missed nothing as he skim-read the early-morning edition of the *Kalahari Times*, printed in the sand.

Jolyon had brought us to a part of the reserve frequented by a large pride of lions, so we needed to be more cautious than usual. Driving up a steep dune, William raised his hand and Jolyon slowed to let him drop from his seat on the bonnet. He walked off at a tangent, carrying no weapon, secure in his bush knowledge. We parked on the dune crest. It offered spectacular views across Tswalu. The red sand road was a ruler line to the horizon, bisecting a sea of blond grass and camelthorn trees. While Jolyon made coffee on the bonnet, William could be seen on a distant dune, hunting back and forth for spoor. After fifteen minutes, he returned with the briefest shake of his head.

We downed our coffee and pressed on. Jolyon hadn't driven more than a hundred metres when William held up his hand again. Tracks. We got out and gathered round. I could clearly see the five digits of the hind feet, the intermittent scrape marks of the tail and the occasional indentations of the forelimbs, which pangolins mostly keep clear of the ground while walking. William took a walkie-talkie from the console and strode off following the spoor, while Jolyon and I drove in a square pattern to see whether the animal had crossed up ahead.

A call came through on the walkie-talkie. William had found a promising burrow. Jolyon grabbed his rifle and we walked over a dune to where William stood beside an aardvark hole. Jolyon got down on his hands and knees, shining a torch into the mouth. "I'm scared of two things when I put my head down a hole: angry snakes or the burrow collapsing on me," he said. "You two better be ready to pull me out by my legs, hey."

Jolyon levered himself in, head first, and soon only his feet showed above ground. Down the rabbit hole, just like Alice, I thought. After a few moments, he backed out, his body coated in red sand. "It goes very deep, and turns a corner," he said, taking out his GPS and marking the coordinates. "I think he's down there. We could try to dig him out, but that's unethical. He's not likely to budge during the day and will probably emerge after sunset to forage. Let's return this evening and stake it out."

Back at the hole after an early supper, the spoor told us our pangolin had already left the burrow. My spirits sank. I was surprised at how each promising sign or disappointment had begun to affect me.

"Damn it," muttered Jolyon. "They hardly ever appear before sunset, and never on a hot summer's day. What's with this guy? We'll just have to try and follow the tracks."

This was going to be a severe test of William's skill. Following the spoor of the Kalahari's most elusive mammal, at night, through tall grass, was surely a bridge too far, even for the finest of trackers. Nevertheless, we set off into the darkness behind William. Our soft-spoken guide seemed to be in his element. He would walk a little way, backtrack, stand thinking for a while, then head off in a different direction altogether, as though somehow divining pangolin. It was fascinating to watch him and Jolyon at work. Not a word was spoken. The merest nod or hand gesture was enough as they zigzagged across the dunes.

I followed them at a distance as they traced a series of loose circles, playing their torches across the ground. I tried to spot the vague indentations that William identified as pangolin spoor, but saw nothing. This was tracking of the highest order. A herd of puffy clouds drifted overhead and obscured the moon, turning the sky to grey tortoiseshell. The air was filled with the shrill monotone of crickets, the Morse chipping of geckos. I tried not to think about lions.

The paucity of tracks, given the abundance of grass, was making it almost impossible for William to keep on the spoor. "Let's follow him in the vehicle," said Jolyon. "You drive, I'll sit on the bonnet. The desert around here is full of aardvark holes, so be careful. We don't want to snap an axle."

I eased the Land Rover into gear and set off after William at a crawl. Jolyon gave hand directions from the jockey seat. It was a matter of continuously weaving between low thorn trees and aardvark burrows, which seemed to gape threateningly at every turn. We spent hours doing this, but with no luck.

The rest of my time at Tswalu followed the routine of early morning and night-time searches. We found plenty of tracks, and Jolyon stuck his head down many a scary hole, but the pangolins remained aloof. On my last day at Tswalu, we embarked on one final, concerted hunt. Among the dune streets to the west of Motse, in the shade of a line of silver cluster-leaf trees, William again found tracks, and we followed them to a burrow.

Both men assured me the pangolin was definitely in residence. This time we weren't taking any chances. We would return long before sunset to stake out the hole.

Later that day, we were back. While William kept an eye on the burrow, Jolyon laid out a fancy picnic supper of roast beef, kebabs and salad, washed down with chilled Windhoek lagers. We sat in camp chairs watching the afternoon bleed into a fiery sunset. Jolyon spoke about growing up in suburban Sasolburg, his flight from the city and his twelve years in the bush, mostly at Madikwe Game Reserve in North West Province, a transitional zone between Kalahari and Bushveld.

Turtle doves trilled the air. Korannaberg Mountain turned salmon, then purple. Supper finished, we went to relieve William. Jolyon and I found comfortable patches of sand near the mouth of the burrow. We remained completely silent, willing the creature to poke its nose above ground. A full moon rose, drenching us in pseudo-sunlight. A wildebeest snorted close by. Lightning flashed on the horizon, too far away to offer any thunder. The moon unpicked itself from a thorn tree. Jolyon chewed a piece of grass. I tried to jot notes by the light of the moon, but soon gave up. Hours dragged by and the sand grew uncomfortable. Was our quarry really down there, or had it slipped out during a moment of inattention?

Eventually, in the early hours of the morning, we gave up. I was more frustrated than I dared show. Maybe the pangolin had foraged well the day before and didn't need to emerge that night. Perhaps it had heard us and decided to lie doggo. The stakeout was a big let-down, and Jolyon appeared visibly disappointed. "I'm a professional," he grumbled. "I should be able to get this little guy."

"Don't cut yourself up about it," I said. "They're supposed to be just about impossible to see. There's a good reason why no-one tracks them."

"Ja, I know, but still—"

Next morning, Jolyon and William escorted me to the main gate, where we got out of our respective Land Rovers and shook hands. "Good luck finding your damn pangolin!" called Jolyon as I pulled off down the long sandy road back to Hotazel.

It took four hours of desert driving to reach my next destination, a game ranch situated between the Northern Cape towns of Kuruman and Upington. At the end of a long, stony gravel track, I came to the imposing gates of Kalahari Oryx, a private hunting estate the size of a small country. The lodge itself, when it hove into view, sported Hobbit-like, thatched towers ostensibly inspired by rhino horns, but looking more like witches' hats.

I turned off just before reaching the lodge and pulled up in front of the low, sprawling manager's house. My arrival was announced by a posse of barking Jack Russells. For the coming days, I'd be staying with the family of ranch manager Errol Pietersen. His son, Darren, was an MSc student at Pretoria University doing ground-breaking research on the ecology and physiology of pangolins in arid environments.

A barefoot Darren met me in the driveway. A tall, shy twenty-something with a gentle demeanour, he led me to a guest room that normally houses overflow hunters from the main lodge. "Come through for supper with the family at seven, and then we'll go get you a pangolin," he said.

I unpacked and settled in. The eaves outside my window were home to a colony of sociable weavers, which had built their haystack-like nest around the corner of the house. Grey, non-descript birds, en masse they're formidable creatures. When they were active, which was most of the time, it sounded as though my room was in the heart of the nest. Given the cacophony, it was clear there were extensive renovations in progress, complete with engineers, clients and contractors squabbling over materials and time frames, aperture placement and predator security measures. The sounds varied from raspy chiii-shhh-shhh emissions to staccato metallic chipping, and from descending trills to apocalyptic chiii-chichichichi explosions. It was hard to think, let alone write.

At supper, I met Darren's parents. Michèle, an attractive redhead, dished homemade lasagne while her husband poured the wine. With his rectangular moustache, erect posture and precise demeanour, Errol had the air of a Victorian colonel from the Queen's Guard. Conversation was lively, and it soon became apparent that Darren's love of nature was inherited from his father. The man was an idealist who spoke ardently about global warming and conservation, a future Earth with twelve-billion souls, the curse of religions, and the coming wars over natural resources such as water. His attitudes were uncompromising, his delivery compelling. In his view, we humans were the aggressors, and it was up to us to make things right.

Before coming to the Kalahari, the Pietersens had lived in the Kruger Park, where Errol was a section ranger for much of Darren's childhood. Thereafter, the family had spent a few happy years in Mozambique's Banhine National Park, where Errol was a technical adviser. During his free time, he'd found three species that were possibly new to science. The young Darren had learnt from a formidable teacher.

The Pietersens then moved to the Northern Cape, where Errol took up his current post as manager of Kalahari Oryx, an exclusive lodge catering mostly to wealthy foreign hunters. At five-hundred-and-forty square kilometres, it's one of the largest pieces of private land in southern Africa, and provides habitat for a number of endangered species. Errol was not in favour of hunting, and his job largely kept him away from that aspect of ranching. He did, however, have to stock a much wider diversity of game than would naturally have occurred there, in order to satisfy the hunters' thirst for variety.

"We need to be careful not to mix some of our hunting clients," he said. "Like when we had heavy-drinking

American and Russian parties at the same time, all armed to the teeth. I thought we were in for round two of the not-so-Cold War."

After supper, I flipped through the hunting magazines on the coffee table while Darren got ready for our own hunt. There were countless photographs of men posing with rifles beside animals they'd shot, often with an affectionate hand on the corpse. All had beaming smiles—the elation of the kill. There were even pictures of wives and children posing with their bloodied prey. It's an odd business that I'll never properly fathom. I know the financial arguments for controlled hunting, but can't accept the sordid business of killing for trophies and pleasure.

Darren finished loading up his research vehicle, a sponsored Mazda pick-up sporting "Pangolin Working Group" stickers on the doors. With telemetry, spotlights and warm clothes on board, we headed out. While Darren had been quiet over supper, deferring to his father, he now became talkative. There was the same passion for the land, the same intensity, just in a younger form. As we drove, he spoke about his thesis. "Originally I wanted to return to Mozambique and do a project in Banhine, but the funding and the vehicle fell through. So I started looking closer to home. We'd had a few pangolin sightings at Kalahari Oryx, so it was a natural choice. Very little research has been done on them, especially these western pangolins. Over time, I became more and more fascinated. They're such mysterious creatures."

He told me about the pioneering work done by

Jonathan Swart in and around the Kruger Park during the 1990s. Darren was comparing those earlier findings with his own observations of "desert" pangolins. Most noticeably, they were on average a third smaller than those studied by Swart, and had adapted in many ways to the drier conditions. In the Kalahari, their home ranges were a lot larger, and they were diurnal in winter, unlike their lowveld cousins.

Darren told me he was recording everything from metabolic rates and body temperature to dispersion of young animals and home-range dimensions. At the moment, he was assessing diet by direct observation, but would soon be moving onto scat study and stomach-content analysis of the dead animals he'd found. Darren sent samples to Pretoria Zoo, where he was involved in a population genetic study to see how the DNA from Kalahari pangolins differed from eastern pangolins. Ideally, they wanted samples from across southern Africa to ascertain whether the various populations were still linked, whether there was movement between them, and how genetically distinct they were. We drove along red sand roads hemmed by walls of white grass. The pick-up rose and dipped like a boat negotiating Kalahari waves. We stopped beside a waterhole to watch two magnificent porcupines drinking, their cloaks of black-and-white quills shimmering in the headlights. Later, Darren had to slam on brakes to avoid a skunk snoozing in the middle of the road.

"My dad used to keep those guys as pets," said Darren. "We've got a few that regularly come and steal the dogs' food. The little rascals troop through the house as if they own it. They know they've got this terrible biological weapon, so they're not exactly shy. One of our Jack Russells messed with one a few nights ago, and we haven't let her in the house since. It's the dog box for her until the pong goes away."

Every now and then we halted on the lip of a dune so Darren could check his telemetry. When the transmitter began ticking loudly, we parked and gathered the gear. Darren thrust his revolver into a holster, and we continued on foot, following the pulse into the darkness. It was cold, and Darren pulled on an old jacket whose sleeves were shredded. I asked him what had happened to it.

"Oh, a blue wildebeest got hold of it," he said.

"While you were in it?"

"Ja, at the time I was, actually."

"Not his colour?"

"No, didn't fit him either, despite the arm alterations. So I got it back."

The telemetry's bleating grew stronger. I was excited and strangely nervous. I'd waited so many years for this. My very first pangolin. This animal, more than any other, was the symbol of my impossible quest. I thought of all my fruitless pursuits over the years. Could this be the moment?

We came to a burrow, and Darren pointed his Yagi antenna at the ground. The creature was down there somewhere. "Very odd," said Darren. "It's already ten o'clock and he hasn't come out yet. Maybe the full moon is keeping him underground."

I imagined Mr Pangolin in his comfortable home beneath our feet. If I crawled into the hole, would it fall away into a long shaft lined with bookshelves and maps of the Kalahari? Would I, like Alice, end up in a room with a table and a little bottle with a label that read "drink me"? And would the drinking of it make me shrink to a size that allowed me to enter Mr Pangolin's study, where I'd find him sitting in an overstuffed armchair sipping a G&T and reading the *Encyclopaedia Britannica*?

"Come, let's go find another burrow," said Darren. We set off across the luminous veld, the moon bright enough for us to walk by its light. Darren strode ahead, bounding over tussocks of dry grass. I had to trot to keep up. "I've got six pangolins collared. Hopefully this next female will be out foraging."

After fifteen minutes we reached another hole. It was the same story. She was under our feet, deep in the chambers of an aardvark burrow. I could imagine her there, curled in a ball, tail wrapped around her head, body temperature lowered, deep in blissful slumber. Or perhaps she was knitting in front of the telly. After the lack of pangolin success at Tswalu, my patience was wearing thin. I fantasised about dropping a fire-cracker down the hole to get her attention. Or even a hand grenade. I tried to hide my frustration.

Darren looked perplexed. "This doesn't normally happen. Maybe they heard you were coming."

"Thanks," I said. "I normally only have that effect on *Homo sapiens* females. Now what?"

"Er, let's go home and hang out for a few hours, then try again."

After midnight, we returned to find both pangolins still ensconced in their lodgings. "I just can't figure this out," said Darren as we returned to the vehicle. "Better luck tomorrow night."

We drove back to the homestead and I climbed into bed feeling thwarted and irritable. It was though I was in a battle with enemy pangolins that refused to show themselves. Almost immediately, a shrill whistle sounded. I opened my eyes and climbed the ladder—over the top and into a hail of bullets. On either side were lines of men running towards the barbed wire. Through swirling smoke we saw the machine guns spitting from a line of foxholes. The pangolins were cutting down our ranks with withering fire. I dived into a shell crater as lead filled the air above my head.

Then we heard the terrifying sound of armour. A single giant pangolin lumbered towards us out of the smoke, its scales clanking above the din of battle. A long tongue of flame spat from its muzzle. The monster was heading straight for our hole, bent on crushing us. I crouched down, hugging my rifle and pulling the tin hat over my eyes. At the last instant, the creature sheered away.

Suddenly I was consumed by rage. I stood up and ran at the enemy, yelling at the top of my lungs. Others were sprinting forward. The enemy fire faltered. Some pangolins turned to run and were cut down. Within moments, I was past the first foxholes. On we ran, until we reached the bunkers. The pangolins were down there, cowering in their stinking burrows. I found a ventilation shaft and dropped in two grenades. There was a scream, then a muffled harrumph. The ground shook beneath my feet. No one's getting out of there alive. There'll be pangolin stew for dinner tonight. Bang, crash, scrape, the twitter of weaver birds. Scuffle. The tawoo of an owl; silence. I floated back into disembodied slumber.

I spent the next morning sitting on a private terrace, catching up my notes. The sociable weavers soon took me for just another piece of furniture, and flapped about unconcerned. Their wings sounded like the purring of a cat on steroids. At one point, I looked up from my journal to see a pair of white rhinos approaching to eat from a drum of feed. Their horns had been sawn off to protect them from poachers. They eyed me warily as they munched, then sauntered off down the road.

I was thinking about the Pietersens. They were a completely integrated bush family. Skunks in the living room, weavers colonising the roof, rhinos on the front lawn... and dead pangolins in the deep freeze (for dissection purposes, Darren explained). Their shelves were crammed with books on fauna and flora, a stuffed black eagle perched in the living room, presiding over discussions that ranged from natural history to ecology and conservation. Having grown up in the Kruger, and with a father like Errol, Darren's bush knowledge was almost a kind of instinct. When we walked in the night-time veld, he'd mention details of the spoor we encountered as though reading roadside billboards. These things were not learnt, but rather osmosed since birth.

After lunch, I joined Darren for a drive to check on his sleeping pangolins. The ranch was vast: from the main lodge to one of the western camps was a distance of forty kilometres. Our circuit gave me a chance to see the diversity of terrain and view the many species kept in various encampments, from rhino and sable antelope to bontebok and red hartebeest.

Driving along, Darren chatted about pangolins. He estimated there were about sixty on the property, although a number had recently been killed by the electric fences. Other than humans, such fences are the only real threat to pangolins. When they get shocked, they automatically roll into a ball for self-defence, often around the electrified strand, which then repeatedly shocks the animal. Some have learnt to adapt; however, many are still killed this way. "We're busy experimenting on the farm with fences that allow for pangolin traffic," said Darren.

Humans are the creature's principal enemy. Apart from habitat loss through development and farming, pangolins are also used in traditional medicine and considered a delicacy in the Far East. With the rapid decline in the four Asian species, foreigners are moving in on the African species. Local threats are just as serious. For instance, in traditional Shona culture, any pangolin found is to be killed and presented to the chief: only he is allowed to eat such a delicacy. Darren said you could buy individual pangolin scales at Johannesburg's muti markets for less than £5 a piece. "Witchdoctors are very keen on them. We notice evidence of the trade with road kill," he said. "If you don't pick up the body of a pangolin immediately when you spot one, it will have disappeared in a couple of hours."

He talked about the African Pangolin Working Group he'd become involved in. It's led by a number of conservationists and scientists from many fields seeking to ascertain what preservation measures are needed for all four African species. The group is mapping distribution and trying to establish biological factors such as physiology, reproductive biology, home range and habitat use. As Darren talked, we drove from hole to hole determining with telemetry who was in residence and who was on walkabout. By the time we got back to the house, both of us were hot, tired and dusty.

Over supper, Errol confided some of the difficulties of ranching with wild animals in the midst of a livestock farming region. "We're sometimes not very popular with the locals, especially when a big cat escapes," he said. "One of our lions recently killed a cow. Fortunately, on that occasion the farmers didn't mind so much because it was generally agreed that the cow had been taunting the lion on the other side of the electric fence, and had got its just desserts. The lion was driven so mad with frustration that it simply charged through the fence. But there have been other, less legitimate, incidents."

Errol didn't elaborate. He went on to speak about the close-knit farming communities of the Kalahari, and how they stuck together, especially in times of crisis. For instance, everyone got together to help fight fires. Farmers would come from hundreds of kilometres away to lend a hand. It was also a chance to gossip and drink lots of brandy. "Get-togethers sometimes get out of hand," said Errol. "One of the more dangerous pastimes is to take a motorbike and ride alongside a running gemsbok, leap across and grab the antelope by its horns. Alcohol, as you might surmise, is usually involved. One farmer even managed to get a gemsbok horn stuck through his chin and out his cheek. It's all jolly good fun."

Hunting is extremely popular in the Kalahari. Many locals have chairs with seatbelts mounted on the back of their pick-ups, and charge through the veld chasing anything on four legs. If they ever catch sight of a jackal or caracal, all work stops immediately, and everyone grabs rifles and shotguns to take up the chase in vehicles or on horseback. "If necessary, they'll hunt an animal for days, until they've killed it," said Errol. "But make no mistake, these farmers also have hearts of gold. They're the salt of the earth. The toughest, kindest people you'll ever meet."

Conversation turned to white lions, and Errol expressed his disapproval at their presence on my Impossible Five list. "Those damn cats shouldn't be given so much publicity. It just encourages people to breed more of them for zoos and circuses. Why don't you go for something like a black-footed cat instead?"

"Not sexy enough," I said. "My list is very personal. There are plenty of mammals, even from this area, that could've made the cut. I mean, why not the Namaqua mole-rat?"

"Oh, you'll never ever find one of those," he scoffed.

"The De Beers diamond miners find them all the

94

time," I said. "Well, bits of them at least, when they're blasting. They keep mistaking them for flying squirrels."

The corner of Errol's mole-rat-shaped moustache quivered with the vaguest suggestion of a smile.

After supper, Darren and I loaded the pick-up and headed out once more into the star-splattered Kalahari night. Coming round a bend we surprised a young porcupine, which set off at a helter-skelter run, but stayed in the sandy groove of a tyre track. We slowed to let it get ahead of us and find an escape route. On and on it ran, never leaving the track. We stopped and switched off the headlights for a while to give the creature a chance to orientate itself. Driving again, we soon caught up with it, still jogging along in the groove.

"I suppose it wouldn't be politic to run the thing over," I said.

"Better not, the quills might puncture our tyres," said Darren. It was some minutes before we could induce the porcupine to get out of the way. On we drove, into a night filled at every quadrant with bounding bunnies. We identified scrub hares, spring hares and Cape hares but, alas, no sign of riverine rabbit. Which was a pity, as this creature was just as impossible as pangolin. It would have been nice to bag two for the price of one.

Darren stopped the vehicle and we walked to the first burrow. Sure enough, the pangolin was still underground. It was *déjà vu*. We walked to the second burrow—and found the same scenario. By now I'd kind of resigned myself to the disappointment, but Darren was perplexed.

We returned to the vehicle and drove in silence to a distant burrow belonging to one of the western pangolins. Darren parked beside a windmill whose shattered blades were enveloped by a sociable weaver nest. It looked as though a haystack had flown into it at high speed. We climbed a hill and arrived at the hole. The little scoundrel inside was also fast asleep.

There comes a time in every unsuccessful quest when one's equanimity begins to resemble a very old, very frayed rope, and just then I had a clear picture of the flimsy strand of hemp that was mine. Had there been a spade handy, I might well have done a spot of exploratory digging. Or used a hand grenade. I feared that my frustration was about to boil over, which would have been unfair on Darren, who was doing his best.

The night wore on as we checked the other burrows. Four hours had passed, and it was well past midnight. I'd given up all hope by the time we dragged our weary feet to the last candidate's hole. Darren directed his torch beam at a clump of grass.

And there he was, in plain sight, not five metres away. My heart may well have stopped beating for a few delicious moments. At last, the very symbol of my quest. I stared in astonished, delirious wonder.

The pangolin waddled across our path, a scraping sound coming from his scales. Tokman was an adult male of about ten kilograms. He emitted a low purring, a quieter version of an elephant's rumble. The creature looked like a cross between a pinecone and a sausage dog. I was both entranced and elated; Darren seemed visibly relieved.

"Do you know how old he is?" I whispered.

"Not sure. He's certainly a mature chap. The books say pangolins live up to twelve years, but I'm convinced that's wrong. Given their slow reproductive rate—one pup a season—and the fact that they only reach maturity after three years, I'm sure they live a lot longer. It's so cute: the babies actually ride on their mothers' backs like jockeys."

We drew closer and watched Tokman foraging for ants. He blew gently through his thin, delicate nose to clear sand from the tunnels, then probed with a sticky tongue for ants, pupae and larvae. After less than a minute he moved on, as the bites of the defending ants grew too uncomfortable.

"In Afrikaans, a pangolin is an *ietermagog*, which probably refers to its food," whispered Darren. "A *machocho* is an ant in Tswana."

"He's so calm. Can't he see us?" I asked, hardly daring to blink lest he disappear.

"Pangolins have lousy vision," said Darren. "They sniff and bump their way around the veld. When it's time to go back to their dens, they follow their own scent trails home."

I stepped forward to take a photograph and stumbled on a clump of grass. At last Tokman heard us and immediately rolled up, pressing his nose to his chest, tucking in his legs and pulling his tail around his body. In this posture, he looked like an armoured soccer ball. Darren picked him up carefully, keeping his hands well clear of the tail that scythed back and forth. If you allowed a finger to get caught beneath the scales, it could be cut to the bone. Once a pangolin has rolled into a ball, it's almost impossible for predators to get at them. Lions' teeth can penetrate individual scales, but these are layered in such a way that carnivores struggle to get a grip.

Peering beneath a gap in the armour, I could make out an adorable little face, pink and pointy with pinprick eyes. It was the face of a very old man. I was transfixed. While I gazed into those ancient eyes, Darren checked his transmitter, which was bolted onto the animal like a backpack. Each time I touched Tokman, his tail scythed viciously. I ran my fingers along his flank: the scales were hard like plastic, more reptilian than mammalian. The pangolin was unlike any creature I'd ever encountered; it was as though I were touching a living fossil.

While I sat watching a curled-up Tokman, Darren took GPS coordinates, gathered samples of the ants he'd been feeding on, and jotted notes about behaviour. After a while, Tokman grew more confident and half unravelled himself to see what was what.

We backed off downwind to an unobtrusive distance. Within a minute, he'd plucked up enough courage to unravel completely, his scales clicking in the still night air. Then Tokman waddled noisily into the night with a rocking gait, a prehistoric beetle shambling off in the blaze of a full Kalahari moon. It was a scene that has hardly changed in forty-million years.

Quinton Martins employs a UHF aerial to get a GPS fix for Max, a collared leopard cruising the slopes of Sneeuberg.

Bushnell   08-06-2010 12:28

Infrared-camera traps are Quinton's permanent 'eyes on the ground' in the Cederberg and provide invaluable images of leopards. Picture: Cape Leopard Trust.

Fred Dalerum is a nutty Swedish zoologist researching aardwolves, bat-eared foxes and aardvarks on Benfontein Farm outside Kimberley.

William Gatsene and Jolyon Neytzell-de-Wilde make a formidable tracking team at Tswalu Game Reserve in the southern Kalahari.

Down the rabbit hole. Well, not quite. Jolyon takes a peek inside a vacant aardvark manor: no one home, again.

With bunny ears and a Hoover snout, the less charitable might describe the aardvark as a cross between a pig, a rabbit and a toilet brush.

The southern African ground pangolin is a prehistoric-looking creature whose body is covered in an armour of brown scales, making it appear more dinosaur than mammal. Picture: Jolyon Neytzell-de-Wilde.

Darren Pietersen uses telemetry to check on the whereabouts of his beloved pangolins.

Darren keeps his fingers clear of Tokman the pangolin's scything tail (note the transmitter, bolted onto the animal like a small backpack).

The piratical, red-bearded Keir Lynch has a soft spot for the riverine rabbit, which he describes as the Porsche of bunnies.

With white rings around the eyes, like spectacles that make it look vaguely professorial, and a black stripe extending below the mouth to give it an uncertain smile, the riverine rabbit is the rarest mammal in Africa. Picture: Keir Lynch.

A female leopard at Motswari Game Reserve slinks through the dusky bushveld to retrieve her hidden impala kill.

Tracker Tiyani Mashele and field guide Shadrack Mkhabela set their sights on finding a white lion at Motswari.

Marah the white lion is flanked by her protectors, Jason Turner and Linda Tucker, at Tsau Reserve's Unicorn Camp.

Zukhara and Matsieng, with their gorgeous 1970s hairdos, enjoy a lowveld sunrise at Tsau. Picture: Global White Lion Trust.

NO SEX PLEASE, WE'RE RABBITS

Once upon a time, millions of years ago, there lived a family of rabbits in the north of England. They were happy and content, but their world was about to be turned inside out. Winters were growing longer and colder, living conditions harsher. An Ice Age had begun setting in. Peter, the eldest of the rabbit siblings, started looking into the possibility of emigration to Spain, the Algarve or somewhere else with greener grass and a warmer clime. One evening, a family meeting was held in the warren of his mother, Mrs Rabbit. After careful deliberation and lengthy debate, it was decided they should undertake a great trek.

With heavy hearts, they packed all they could carry and bade farewell to their comfy homes in the roots of a grove of fir trees. They left the verdant hills of what would one day be called the Lake District and hopped south. It was a mild spring morning and most of the snow had melted, but they were nonetheless bundled up with rabbit-wool mittens and muffatees. The journey ahead could last many seasons, and they didn't know where they might end up. Peter led the group, with his young cousin Benjamin bounding ahead to spy out the land. They were on the lookout for Tommy the Badger and Mr Tod the Fox, who were both partial to rabbit pie and might be tempted to pick off a straggler if they weren't vigilant. Behind the two leading rabbits came Benjamin's wife Flopsy, her sister Mopsy and their young brood, bounding gaily along. In the rear came Mrs Rabbit, in earnest conversation with Cotton-tail, her youngest.

It took them several months to reach Dover. In those days, England was still conveniently attached to France, so there was no need for the Eurostar. They turned right, traversed the Pyrenees in the spring and found some warmth on the summery plains of Spain. But the cold of another bitter winter drove them south again, where they crossed the Gibraltar land bridge to Africa. Here it was indeed much warmer, and the family could settle down and make a home. They took to wearing jellabiyas and eating dates; Benjamin even acquired a hookah pipe.

Years passed. The offspring of that intrepid band of Europeans adapted to the new land and its scary predators. But they retained many of their European habits: they insisted on making their homes in burrows, and refused to take on the haphazard, above-ground squatting habits of African hares, whom they looked down their snouts at. "One must maintain standards," Mrs Rabbit insisted, and all future generations stuck to her mantra. Over the centuries, this brood of rabbits continued trekking south. Countless thousands of years later they crossed the equator; still more centuries passed, and eventually they arrived in South Africa. Like many British settlers of a later era, they found the Karoo to their liking. One of them even penned a little masterpiece of rabbit fiction entitled *The Story of an African Warren*.

As much of the Karoo is arid, the rabbits stuck to watercourses where they could burrow in the softer sand to make their breeding dens. They became entirely adapted to a riverine environment. Then disaster struck. A new wave of colonists arrived from the cold north. These ones stood on two legs and didn't dig warrens. But they wanted the alluvial land for their farms. Slowly they forced the rabbits out, ploughing up the fertile soil for winter wheat, felling vegetation for wood, damming the streams and letting their livestock graze and trample the riverine lands. Farm workers hunted these slow rabbits with toothy dogs, which further reduced their numbers.

Within three centuries of their arrival at the Cape, the new Europeans had driven the old Europeans to the brink of extinction. At the time of my rabbit quest, it was thought there were as few as two-hundred-and-fifty breeding pairs of riverine rabbits left, making them the most endangered mammal in Africa, and the thirteenth most endangered mammal on earth.

Riverine rabbits are still occasionally spotted in isolated pockets of the Great Karoo and, more recently, in parts of the Little Karoo. But if you want to see one for yourself—and the chances are very slim—the best place to try your luck is Sanbona, two-hundred-and-fifty kilometres northeast of Cape Town. This large wildlife reserve is one of the few places the rabbit still has a halfway decent chance of survival. I contacted a leading scientist in the field, Christy Bragg, and she suggested I visit the area during the new moon, which provided the best opportunity of finding one of these shy, nocturnal animals out in the open. She was also kind enough to bring me up to date on her team's research in the Nama Karoo and the exciting prospects at Sanbona, especially with the introduction of camera traps to develop an understanding of the rabbits' ecological behaviour.

I set off northeast from Cape Town and, after an hour and a half, swung right at Worcester. Entering the Little Karoo, my Land Rover passed through the rock portal of Cogman's Kloof, where an Anglo-Boer War blockhouse stands sentinel above the road. The R62, one of the loveliest roads in the Republic, snaked out of the gorge, through the town of Montagu, with its whitewashed and thatched Cape Dutch buildings, past blossoming apricot and pear orchards, and into the arid mountains to the east. After half an hour, a turn to the north took me onto a gravel road that led towards a mountain range, pale and shimmering in the midday heat. Behind it, stood another taller range—the very ramparts of the Great Karoo. I signed in at the gate and entered Sanbona.

The reserve comprises five-hundred-and-forty square kilometres, made up of nineteen farms that were bought and amalgamated to form the third largest private conservation area in South Africa. Although it's home to the Big Five, Sanbona is also a biodiversity hotspot, and guests are encouraged to take an interest in the flora as much as the fauna. The reserve protects three distinct biomes: the wetter, more fertile renosterveld (a Cape vegetation type favoured by rhinos) of the south, the fynbos-rich Warmwaterberg range that runs from west to east through its centre, and the drier Karoo of the north with its succulent plants.

As I drove to the main lodge, scanning the landscape for any sign of burrows or a fleeting glimpse of a furry body, I was thinking about the countless bunnies of legend and history. Children grow up with a whole range of rabbit characters to fill their young imaginations. From the tales of Beatrix Potter and Lewis Carroll's *Alice in Wonderland* to the trickster Brer Rabbit and the tempestuous bunny society of *Watership Down*. In Aesop's Fables, the hare is often pitted against other animals, such as the wily fox or sluggish tortoise. In cinema, Bugs Bunny remains a favourite and rabbits appear in countless Hollywood movies, from early Disney classics to *Who Framed Roger Rabbit*.

Bunnies have an important place in the folklore of many cultures. They are symbols of fertility and rebirth, often associated with spring (Christianity's pagan Easter bunny) and, given their reputation for procreation, with sexuality and reproduction. Rabbits abound in the tales and belief systems of ancient societies. In Aztec mythology, a pantheon of rabbit gods represented a kind of bacchanalian fertility. The rabbit is one of the twelve celestial animals in the Chinese Zodiac, while in Japanese tradition a bunny lives in the moon. In Jewish folklore, rabbits are associated with cowardice, while in Native American Ojibwe mythology, the Great Rabbit helped create the world.

Driving north, mulling over my quest to find an almost impossible rabbit, I felt a bit like a ham-fisted fox chasing a flighty hare in a fairy-tale of my own devising. The bunnies I knew from childhood books and cartoons were happy to remain just out of reach and drive their pursuers crazy. Would the riverine rabbit play ball or lead me on an endless fruitless chase?

Daydreaming as I drove, I imagined that a cast of rabbit characters had joined me in the car and were behaving badly on the back seat. I pictured a troop of Beatrix Potter's bunnies quarrelling with a bunch from *Watership Down*. The Easter rabbit sat primly with a basket of colourful eggs on her lap, trying to mind her own business. A tortoise and a hare were doing stretching exercises on the back windowsill and eyeing each other. Brer Rabbit shouted above the hubbub, trying to recount a tale of how he'd got the better of a shotgun-wielding farmer and had taught him a lesson he'd never forget. A white rabbit wearing a waistcoat sat beside him, but didn't say a word to the uncouth American. "I say, do hurry up driver, we're going to be late," he chided.

The road traversed stony ground dotted with wild flowers in acid shades of yellow, pink and scarlet. Springbok and gemsbok grazed on distant slopes. The road snaked through a series of gorges, dwarfed by the contorted rocks of the Warmwaterberg, tousled and rumpled like sandstone bedclothes. At last the terrain opened out into a valley carpeted with purple flowers. On its eastern slope stood a homestead shaded by eucalyptus trees. The rabbits in the back quietened down and peered over my shoulder as we approached.

"Is that a farmhouse, like with a farmer, like with a gun?" squeaked Brer Rabbit.

"Yes it is," I said.

In a flash, all the bunnies vanished.

I parked under the bluegums and got out. Tilney Manor dates from the 1890s, and is today the main lodge of Sanbona. It's a typical, double-storey, flat-roofed Karoo house with a pediment and glassed-in veranda. The antique-filled interiors are cool and dark with high ceilings and creaky floors. The guest rooms are set in a walled garden around a swimming pool. It's a green oasis of Karoo plants, loud with birdsong and smaller wildlife. I thought of the enchanted garden in *Alice and Wonderland*, that manicured Oxford collegiate realm of Lewis Carroll's imagination. Tilney's seemed to me an African equivalent.

As I was led to my room by Jerome, a boomslang sailed past us across the lawn. Instantly, a squadron of wagtails and Cape robins swooped down on it, kicking up an enormous commotion. Boomslangs are one of the most venomous snakes in Africa, but very shy and not likely to harm humans. "Oh dear, that's Smiley being given a hard time by the birds again," chuckled Jerome as he laboured under the burden of my duffel bag and camera equipment. "He's an old resident. Don't worry about him. He's got enough on his plate with those birds."

The snake reared its head and feigned a strike, but the twittering irritants were too fast for him. With an indignant swish, he disappeared behind a botterboom beside the door to my room.

The lodgings were luxurious, with private verandas giving onto veld decked with pink doublaarvygies. The vistas stretched towards a row of green and ochre hills. There was a four-poster bed, fireplace and Victorian bath. If it took me a very long time to find the riverine rabbit, there'd be no hardship involved.

At lunch, I met Keir Lynch, assistant wildlife manager of Sanbona, and a man with a thing for riverine rabbits. He was tall, with a fiery red beard tapering to a point. Of Irish extraction, his pale complexion had burned red under the harsh Karoo sun. The whole effect was somewhat piratical.

"Aaargh, they're magic little animals, them riverines. Sleek, beautifully built: the Porsche of rabbits," enthused Redbeard in a booming voice, as he adjusted his eye patch and called for more grog (or is that my faulty memory?). "We know so little about them and they may all have disappeared before we know much more. Worst-case scenario is that they'll be extinct within our lifetime."

As we tucked into fish and chips, he gave me the lowdown on their plight. Riverine rabbits are critically endangered largely because their natural habitat of soft alluvial soils for easy digging is so limited; it's also shrinking all the time due to farming activity and the fragmentation of suitable land. The situation has been exacerbated by jackal-proof fencing which hems in isolated populations. It's terribly bad luck that these animals require exactly the same environment as humans.

To make matters worse, they buck the trend of mating like... well... rabbits. By contrast, European rabbits (modern ones, not million-year-old ones) were introduced onto Robben Island by early sailors to provide meat for ships passing the Cape. Today, expensive culling programmes are required to keep the numbers down. However, riverine rabbits are slow breeders, producing only one or two kittens and only one birthing per season. Attempts at captive breeding have been unsuccessful.

"They're actually the only digging rabbits in Africa," Keir explained.

"Like early colonists trying to farm an unforgiving land," I said.

"Ja. But they toughed it out, kept their burrowing habits, stuck to watercourses, went completely nocturnal for safety. Adapt or die, know what I mean. Now, like threatened settlers, they're having their prized alluvial land invaded by a new bunch of farmers."

"Poor bunnies. It's almost Zimbabwean."

"Sort of. They came south down the continent over the millennia and finally reached the Great Karoo. Those that got left behind were probably killed off. Most of our endemic bunnies are actually hares. Think of the Cape hare or the scrub hare. They utilise cover for protection and they don't burrow. And unlike hares, riverine-rabbit young are completely dependent on their mothers after birth. They're blind, they suckle, they've got no hair.

That's why the level of protection needs be so much greater. They have to be underground."

Keir said that in the Cape, conservation areas have traditionally been declared on land unsuitable for farming, so rabbit habitats have not been preserved. Species that are highly adapted to one specific environment are invariably the most at risk. Any change in their eco-system can pose a threat to their survival. The way Keir explained it, the odds were heavily stacked against this little creature.

Research on riverine rabbits began at Sanbona in 2006. They were a recent discovery in the area, and scientists were surprised to find them in the Little Karoo, south of the Great Escarpment. To date, not much is known about this southern population, and how it occupies the renosterveld habitat. Since 2006, more rabbit sightings have been reported by the public in other remote areas of the Cape. They are still listed as critically endangered, but these isolated finds are encouraging.

Keir also talked about the vision for Sanbona. Seeing that all of the Big Five, save for a few reclusive leopards, were long ago shot by farmers, it was the intention of the founders of the reserve to reintroduce much of the game that would once have roamed the Little Karoo. "It's ongoing, pioneering work," said Keir. "For instance, we already have white rhinos; now we want to reintroduce black rhinos from Namibia. They would definitely have occurred here in the old days. But what will the effect on the vegetation be, and how will they adapt their diet to our plants? It's a fascinating process. All our research is ground-breaking. How many elephants would the region have sustained? Would there have been cheetahs here? Even the local riverine rabbits are a bit of a mystery. We don't even know yet if ours are a subspecies."

"Playing God?" I asked.

"Ja, I suppose in a way we are. But also redressing the wrongs of the past. Just think about the slaughter: the first Dutch settlers took just twenty years to shoot all the lions on Table Mountain; twenty-two elephants were killed in the Montagu area in one day; there were leopard traps on every farm. It's a terrible legacy. We're doing things very scientifically here, trying to return a part of the Little Karoo to the way it once was. We're only introducing as many animals as the land can comfortably handle. Our fynbos is just as important as the fauna. I mean, we don't want the ellies trashing everything. We're concerned about the entire eco-system, protecting all three of our biomes in their rich diversity."

That evening marked our first rabbit hunt. It was the new moon, the best time to have a crack at them. However, even in the relative safety of complete darkness, a rabbit in the open is an easy target for the likes of caracal, jackal or owl, and they have to be wary.

Jannie Swanepoel, a young field guide with a freckled, open face, was assigned to me for the duration of my stay. He collected me from the lodge after supper, and we drove to meet Keir in the southern section of the reserve. It was already bitterly cold. We were both bundled under many layers and wore woolly hats and gloves. On the back seat lay hot-water bottles and blankets for later.

The western sky still held the dregs of dusk, but

overhead a river of Karoo stars was beginning to glitter. As we drove, Jannie confessed that he'd only seen riverine rabbits twice during his time at Sanbona. Looking at the terrain, I could see how the low scrub provided ideal cover. A rabbit could be two metres from the vehicle and remain completely hidden.

Jannie told me he'd grown up on a farm in the Free State where he was surrounded by animals, and his parents regularly took in strays and waifs from the wild. The most endearing and problematic house guest was a young porcupine, which the family raised. Even after it was released into the veld, it would return for visits. "He'd scratch at the door to be let in, greet everyone, take a walk around the house, chew a few shoes and have a drink from his water bowl. One day he climbed into the fireplace, scuffed about in the chimney, then walked across my mother's white carpet with sooty feet. She freaked out. He wasn't so welcome after that."

We drew up next to Keir's vehicle, and he climbed into the back of our open Land Cruiser with his spotlights. "No moon, no wind, flipping cold: conditions are perfect for rabbit hunting," said Keir. "Let's do it, me hearties!"

I swept the bush on our left with a spotlight, Keir took the right, and Jannie scanned the road ahead. We drove at tortoise-pace, searching for movement or the tell-tale orange flash of our target's eyes. Keir chatted about rabbits and their popularity in folklore, echoing my imaginings on the drive to the lodge. In Central Africa, Kalulu the Rabbit is a famous joker, always getting the better of his opponents. The Brer Rabbit tales of America can be traced back to slave stories about trickster figures in many parts of Africa. The hare is always quick to pull a prank on other creatures, and is especially fond of making the high and mighty look stupid. It's often been suggested that Brer Rabbit represents the enslaved African who outwits his adversaries, who symbolise white slave owners.

The night grew icy. We tried to ignore the cold that stabbed at every inch of exposed flesh. After a few hours, we all had drinkers' noses and bloodshot eyes. My two companions snared the occasional creature in their beams: an inquisitive jackal, a spotted eagle owl, and a frog both rangers considered "important". My heart wasn't into frogs just then, not even important ones. I needed a bunny and then a warm bed (and not in the Hugh Hefner sense).

It was almost midnight when we stopped to stretch our legs. With shaking hands, Jannie poured not-so-hot water over Nescafé. The coffee almost warmed our insides. The stars were bright enough to illuminate the veld. The scene was magical in its own frosty way.

"When I started monitoring rabbits, I'd pull seven-hour stretches through the night," said Keir. "All on my own. My arms would get muscle spasms from holding up the spotlight. I did five nights in a row before I saw my first rabbit, just a glimpse as it dashed for cover. My best sighting came after a couple of years. The rabbit actually approached me, attracted by the light. I got out the vehicle and it ran around my legs like a tame bunny. I had half an hour with it. Over the moon, I was."

We emptied the tin mugs, stamped our feet a few

times and climbed back into the vehicle. It had become even colder. When we passed through drifts or ravines, the air seemed a solid block of ice that reluctantly transmogrified to let us pass. My left arm had begun to wilt from holding up the spotlight, so I only scanned perfunctorily, no longer darting the beam back and forth or quivering it over likely areas. Eventually, when all of us were frozen stiff, we gave up. Riverine Rabbit 1, Searchers 0.

Back in my room, I crawled under a winter duvet piled high with blankets. Despite my tiredness, I couldn't get to sleep. Lying there, I imagined becoming a character in a childhood tale, an adult version of the fantasy games I once used to play in my head. Wading through a sea of pink flowers, I happened upon a rabbit. Bounding along, it looked almost riverine, but with a paler coat, perhaps an albino. "Oh dear, oh dear, I shall be late!" he muttered. The rabbit stopped, took a tiny cellphone from his waistcoat pocket, looked at the time on the screen, then hurried on. Abruptly, he ducked into a large hole and disappeared.

Without hesitation I followed. The hole went straight for a while, then dipped sharply down, so that I found myself first sliding, then falling into darkness. The hole was very deep and I noticed, as I fell, that the sides were lined with bookshelves. I was falling slowly enough to make out the titles, but too fast to take one out. *The Complete Tales of Peter Rabbit, Aesop's Fables, African Tales of Magic and Mystery.*

I hit the bottom with a bump. Before me lay a long

passage. The pale rabbit was still in sight, hurrying down it. I ran to catch up and heard him say, "Oh my ears and whiskers, how late it's getting. I shall never make it!"

Glancing down, I saw a stable door, about half a metre high, and decided to take a look inside. I turned the key in the lock and got down on my knees to peer in. At the end of a short passage was an enchanted garden filled with the loveliest fynbos I'd ever seen. There were euphorbias and ericas, restios and crassulas. Quiver trees with spiky arms and corpulent botterbooms stood sentinel over beds of Namaqualand daisies. Could this be the rabbit's garden? How I wished I was small enough to squeeze through the passage.

I noticed a bottle on a table with the words "drink me" on the label. So I did, and incredibly my body began to shrink. Soon I was smaller even than the rabbit and became fearful. But I noticed a little cake lying under the table with a label that read "eat me". So I did, and lo and behold, I began to grow again. I grew and grew until my head hit the ceiling. I burst into floods of tears.

Using an ingenious paper fan I'd picked up, I was able to shrink back to normal size, but found that my crocodile tears had created a flood, and I had to make a swim for it. A whole troop of animals was being swept along in the current. Eventually we reached a bank and crawled out. The birds had bedraggled feathers, sodden fur clung to the animals; all were grumpy and uncomfortable. How were we to get dry? The dodo seemed to be a person with some authority, and called out: "Come and sit in a circle, everyone, and I'll tell you something really dry."

We settled ourselves. "Okay folks, ahem, this is the driest thing I know. Why do I call my dog "Cigarette"? Because he has no legs and every night I take him out for a drag."

"Oh no, that's not very dry!" cried the bluebuck. His coat was more black-and-yellow than blue, but I thought this might be part of the joke. The antelope looked very old and moth-eaten, as though he were actually a stuffed ex-buck. "What do you call a deer with no eyes?" he asked in a creaky voice. "No eye-deer!"

"Oh dear, oh dear, that's not dry enough to dry us!" shouted the quagga. She looked like a joke herself, with her zebra head and donkey body. "How about this?" she cried. "What's the difference between chopped beef and pea soup? Everyone can chop beef, but not everyone can pea soup, ha, ha, ha."

By then, I was no longer paying much attention to the banter, but I did feel a little drier.

"Let's have a race!" cried the dodo.

"What sort of race?" asked the bluebuck.

"A Caucus race, of course," said the dodo.

"What's that?" asked the quagga.

"Well, we all race round and round in a circle. It's just so we get warm, see."

"So it's not a race for survival then?" asked the bluebuck.

"No, no, nothing like that."

"Oh good, I've run one of those before, and didn't do too well. Actually, I came stone last."

The dodo rallied everyone and got us trotting in a

circle. After a while, the dodo called out, "Okay, the race is over!"

We gathered round and wanted to know who'd won. The dodo scratched his head. "We've all won!" he said. "We must all get prizes and he will give them to us!" He pointed a shrivelled wing at me.

"No!" I shouted. "You've all lost the race, I'm afraid. There are no winners here. None of you were fit enough."

Eventually, my childlike imaginings put me to sleep.

"Justin, wake up!" There was loud banging on my door. "Cheetahs! Walking past camp, wake up, come quickly!"

It was Jannie. Sleep-befuddled, I rolled out of bed and dragged on some clothes. Three minutes later, I joined him in reception. He loaded a handful of .375 rounds into his CZ rifle, grabbed two water bottles, and we set off at a brisk pace up the valley.

"It's a pair of males," said Jannie. "They've become habituated to humans on foot over the years. If we catch up with them, we might be able to get close."

After half an hour, we spotted the two cats climbing the side of a hill. Jannie picked a route that would cut them off and we hiked into a gorge, scrambled up a rocky incline and topped out just as the cheetahs loped into view. We stood motionless as they approached us head on. I expected them to turn away, but they kept coming. These were powerful adult males, and they were on a mission. Thirty metres, then twenty. I looked at Jannie. He gave the slightest shake of his head. Ten metres. Their mouths were half open as they took short, shallow breaths. The ruffs on the back of their necks stood up. Two knights-errant of the Warmwaterberg. I could hear their raspy breathing. Just when it seemed they'd walk straight into us, they veered and passed within a whisker's breadth, slinking through the fynbos with easy, graceful strides. The trailing cheetah shot a glance in our direction, fixing us for an instant with his golden eyes. Within moments, they'd vanished into a thicket.

That's just the right amount of pre-breakfast adrenalin, I reckoned as we walked back to the manor. Any more and I might have wet my pants.

The ensuing days followed the usual safari-lodge routine: morning game drives, relaxing through the heat of the day in Tilney's garden, and a second game drive or walk in the late afternoon. As I was staying up late on rabbit hunts with Keir and Jannie, I skipped the morning session and slept in.

The game drives and walks gave me a good idea of the environment the rabbits inhabited. Sanbona is one of the few places in the Cape that closely replicates the Little Karoo eco-system as it was before farmers colonised the region. Jannie and I usually headed for the northern part of the reserve, following a winding gorge through the Warmwaterberg, baboons and klipspringers watching our progress from the cliffs. The hills that stretched away to the blue peaks of the Anysberg were full of game, including larger antelope such as eland, kudu and gemsbok. Plains and mountain zebras grazed together, a model of social integration (although, when it came to rolling in the hay, the two species were more old-school and stuck to their own sort).

One afternoon, we happened upon a herd of thirteen elephants browsing in an acacia-woodland thicket. Their flanks caught the last rays of the sun, painting them red. A youngster came over to sniff the bonnet of our vehicle, shook his head with a crack of the ears, then sauntered off to join his mother.

"These are helluva relaxed ellies," said Jannie under his breath. "But they haven't always been like this. One of the matriarchs used to cause us lotsa trouble. I remember this one time she walked right up to the vehicle and tested my face with her trunk. I shat myself. She covered me with her snot. In retrospect, it was one of the most incredible experiences of my life. After that, she was cool with me.

"Another time she came up to the vehicle and went straight for one of my guests in the back. Stuck her trunk in and started feeling his chest. I told everyone to sit dead still. She kept touching him for a long time. Three weeks later, the bloke had a heart attack. She knew, I'm telling you, that ellie just knew. Bloody amazing creatures, hey."

Further up the valley, we found a pair of white rhinos grazing in a field of yellow flowers. Given the insatiable demand for their horns in Asia, rhino poaching is rife everywhere in southern Africa, even in remote Karoo parks. "Some of our anti-poaching patrols have seen cars at night, spotlights in the river bed, a low-flying plane," said Jannie. "So far, Sanbona has been lucky. We haven't lost a rhino yet. But there's so much money in it, the poachers are getting more and more high-tech.

Helicopters, infrared night scopes, you name it. It's a war, and in most places the good guys are losing."

We'd usually halt for drinks on a hill to watch the sunset, then drive slowly back to camp through the dusky veld. On one occasion, we stopped at another lodge, Gondwana, which lies in the centre of the reserve. I was standing on the veranda, minding my own business, when an owl swooped out of the darkness towards me. I ducked, covering my head, my prey instincts kicking in. The bird flared its wings, landed gracefully at my feet and peered up at me with a quizzical look. From its mouth dangled a whipsnake.

"Oh there you two are," said Jannie, emerging from the French doors. "Hello Bubu, how are you, my lovely girl?"

I was, to say the least, surprised. Jannie and the bird were obviously on first-name terms. I was thanking my lucky stars I still had a scalp. "Bubu is a spotted eagle owl, hand-raised by the staff at Gondwana," said Jannie. "She was released a while ago, but she still returns most nights to show off her catch, just like a domestic cat bringing a mouse to its owner. Come say hello, big girl."

Bubu strutted over, her talons clicking on the concrete like high heels. She stood looking up at us with big yellow eyes, the snake swinging back and forth from her bill.

"Go on, you can touch her," said Jannie. "She won't bite."

Of course not, I thought, she hadn't finished hors d'oeuvres yet. I reached down and tentatively stroked the top of her head, feeling the hardness of her skull through coarse feathers.

"Boo, boo," she said.

"Bubu, Bubu, what a good girl you are," said Jannie. "And what a big snake!"

"Boo-boo, boo-boo," said Bubu, more enthusiastically.

"Boo, boo," I replied, getting into the swing of things.

Once she was satisfied we'd made enough fuss over her hunting prowess, she gave a little hop, a couple of wing-beats and dissolved into the night. I wondered if riverine-rabbit Carpaccio ever made it onto her menu.

During the heat of the day, I lay beside the pool with a pile of documents and academic papers that Keir had nudged in my direction. I learnt that my rabbit was first recognised as a new species by a British soldier near De Aar in 1903. Two specimens were sent to the British Museum of Natural History where they were given the name *Bunolagus monticularis*, a "monticule" being a small mountain or hill, which was thought to be their preferred habitat. No further sightings were recorded for many years.

Due to their Latin name, and the fact that they were (incorrectly) classified along with rock rabbits, scientists began searching for them in mountainous terrain. Captain G.C. Shortridge, curator of the Kaffrarian Museum in King William's Town, was a prolific collector of zoological specimens. He took up the hunt in the 1920s, but was unsuccessful. Shortridge became so frustrated that he offered a one-pound sterling reward for any captures, hence the rabbit's old Afrikaans name, pondhaas (pound hare). In 1947, the residents of Calvinia tactfully pointed out to the by now mountainously frustrated Captain Shortridge that he was looking in the wrong places, and should concentrate his search on the alluvium that fringed dry river beds. He was successful straight away, and collected four specimens along the Fish and Rhinoceros rivers in the Eastern Cape.

However, it wasn't until 1978 that a proper research project was undertaken. Scientists from the University of Pretoria were dismayed to find that most of the rabbit's habitat had been ploughed under or overgrazed by small stock. The species was immediately placed on the endangered list, and a study of its ecology begun. By then, it was too late to gain any idea of the original extent of their range. Given their recent discovery in the Little Karoo's renosterveld, it's possible their range extended all the way to Cape Town, but we'll probably never know for sure.

As if mere survival weren't hard enough, I learnt that *Bunolagus monticularis* is also under threat from global warming. As the Karoo hots up through the course of the twenty-first century, its potential habitat will shrink even further. As much as ninety-six percent of its current (already extremely limited) range may be lost. One study sought to develop a habitat model to help find isolated populations that might still exist, as well as to identify suitable areas for their introduction or re-introduction in the future. The paper attempted to map the entire Karoo in terms of where appropriate soil types and plant species that offer good rabbit cover and primary food sources could be found. It appears that in a future, hotter climate, the best chances of survival may be for rabbit populations to migrate or be reintroduced into regions east of their current range.

I trawled through pages and pages of models, statistics and complicated graphs. Admittedly, I nodded off every now and then to the soporific splash of the fountain and chirruping of sunbirds. After short rejuvenating snoozes, I'd press on for a few pages with renewed vigour. I read about unsuccessful captive breeding programmes, and the need for human intervention in order to save *Bunolagus*, or "Bunny Lagos", as I'd taken to calling it.

I let most of the weighty science wash over me, jotting down only the odd nugget. Such as the fact that riverine rabbits raise their young in underground chambers lined with fur and grass, which sounded nice and cosy. Their menu of favourite foods comprised a string of Latin names I didn't recognise, but also local plants like mesembs, boegoe and inkbush, which I did. One academic paper ended on a sobering note: "Given that the population numbers of this species have dipped alarmingly in the last decade, the amount of conservation planning that is still needed and the complications that climate change will introduce, it is suggested that the cryopreservation of genetic material be promoted as a safeguard against the permanent disappearance of this species."

One morning, after a long night of unsuccessful rabbit hunting and a late breakfast, Jannie took me on a walk through the gorge behind Tilney Manor to a San rock-art site. We climbed up the shady side of the cliff through fragrant fynbos until we reached the mouth of the cave. It took a moment for our eyes to adjust in the dim light to the pale ochre figures adorning the walls, but soon we could make out trance-dancing figures, a giraffe, and hunters whirling around a fire. Jannie pointed to a pair of warrior-gatekeepers standing guard over a fissure in the rock that led, perhaps, to the "other side". There were plenty of thumbprints too, probably the marks of ancient initiation rites.

"We think some of these paintings are more than three thousand years old," said Jannie.

"Are there any images of riverine rabbits?" I asked.

"No, unfortunately not. But did you know *Bunolagus monticularis* used to be called the Bushman hare? And rabbits appear regularly in San folklore. For instance, if they killed and ate a hare, they always left a small portion of the meat as an offering and reminder of the time when hares were human."

Jannie went on to recount a San tale, "The Moon, the Hare and the Wedding", in which a hare appears at a wedding and tells the guests that if they don't heed his words, they'll all end up in the underworld when they die. Those who listen to him will enjoy a happy afterlife. He then gives his sermon. Every San should obey the elders and respect the clan. The newlyweds must look after each other all the days of their lives. The community has to live in peace, and everything they own is to be shared equally. "A sermon for us as well as for them, don't you think?" said Jannie.

We sat at the mouth of the cave and gazed into the

valley. The rocks on the opposite slope glistened in the sunshine. Swifts swooped into the cave, their wings droning as they banked in audacious aerobatic displays. I thought of the San who once occupied this place and the rabbit that bore their name. Both had been pushed out by settlers and farmers. Both had been brought to the brink of extinction. But their spirits lived on in remote, dry corners of the Karoo such as this. Although the San were long gone, for riverine rabbits there was still a chance of survival here.

Another night, another bunny hunt. Endless driving, our spotlights stroking the veld, the bushes ever-mesmerising, ever-deceptive. Keir talked about the ongoing rabbit research. At Sanbona, he'd been logging all sightings with GPS, setting up camera traps, monitoring distribution, trying to gauge the success of the southern population and ascertain their favoured vegetation types. By finding out exactly which plants they preferred, scientists would know where in the Little Karoo to look for other isolated populations. They would also be in a position to draw up a habitat-requirement document that could be used by organisations such as the Endangered Wildlife Trust (EWT) and CapeNature to preserve or rehabilitate suitable land.

Sanbona researchers had teamed up with these two conservation bodies for concerted population-survey "hunts", in which a hundred beaters would move through riverine thickets at two-metre intervals, trying to flush out rabbits. Even sniffer dogs were sometimes used to help with the counts, as well as for finding samples of dung, hair and the like. No doubt the dogs would need to be muzzled or extremely well-trained, as the sight of a fleeing rabbit might be too much temptation, even for the laziest and most geriatric of hounds.

This kind of research costs truckloads of money, and sponsors are constantly being sought. For instance, Lindt (the chocolate manufacturer) had been enlisted to use the riverine rabbit for its Easter campaigns, with the EWT receiving a percentage of the profit on each chocolate bunny sold.

"Maybe you should try the *Playboy* route," I suggested. "How about getting Hugh Hefner to sponsor the rarest, sexiest bunny on earth?"

Keir wasn't convinced. We pushed on into the freezing darkness. Hours passed, then more hours. We drove on, but it looked like being another fruitless hunt. I was disappointed, but growing accustomed to the disappointment. Around midnight, Keir suggested turning for home. We'd make one last loop along an overgrown track through a patch of alluvial terrain.

The 4X4 nosed into a gulley, our tyres splashing through a stream. The heady scent of wild lavender filled the air. Keir slowly drew the vehicle to a halt and switched off the engine. "Ah, hello," he said under his breath. "And here on my right, folks, may I present the riverine rabbit."

I was stunned. Just like that, seemingly out of a hat: the riverine rabbit! Adrenalin coursed through me as I fumbled for the camera. The twitching bunny was caught in Jannie's spotlight, about ten metres from the vehicle. I blinked hard a few times to make sure my eyes weren't playing tricks. Once I was over my surprise, and the vague disappointment that this looked a bit like every bunny one has ever seen, I began to take note of its distinctive features.

The rabbit had a coat of tawny umber and was smaller than I'd expected. It had elongated ears with an auburn tinge. Each eye had a white ring, like spectacles, making the rabbit look vaguely professorial. A black stripe extended just below the mouth almost to the ears, giving it a big, if uncertain, smile. All its colours glowed in the spotlight beam. Upon reflection, and closer inspection, it was a very fine-looking bunny indeed.

I glanced at my companions. Their faces were rapturous, like courtiers in the presence of royalty. "A magnificent rabbit, hey," whispered Keir. "Nothing from the photos prepares you for such beauty."

The creature took a few hops. Judging by Keir's expression, it might as well have been the prima ballerina at the Bolshoi. The rabbit ran onto the road in front of the car, our luck holding. Now it was in our headlights, bounding away from us down the track. Keir started the engine and followed slowly. The bunny stopped, turned to look at us, staring straight into our lights, then hopped back towards the vehicle. Its shadow was enlarged by the lights, creating a huge, ghostly figure. I was caught between trying to take photos and wanting to watch. Eventually I put the camera down in favour of savouring the moment. The rabbit bobbed past my side of the vehicle and dived into a bush. Gone.

The stars sang in their icy firmament as we drove home. All three of us had bunolagus grins, me most of all. It was going to take me a while to process the fact that I had just seen the rarest mammal in Africa.

I stayed on an extra day at Sanbona to wrap up my rabbit readings and notes. It gave me a chance to digest my experience. The last riverine rabbits were fortunate indeed to have people like Keir and Jannie, who cared so passionately about them. The researchers, rangers and scientists attached to Sanbona, CapeNature and the EWT have a shared vision for a functional, healthy Karoo ecosystem and suitable socio-economic conditions that can support a stable population of rabbits. These creatures will only survive through habitat conservation, especially of the region's fragile rivers. Preserving the biodiversity, dealing with the threats of solar and wind farms and fracking, as well as encouraging landowners to participate in conservation: all these are vital. As small populations are vulnerable to environment changes, ecological catastrophes and inbreeding, corridors between cut-off populations must be created for the long-term viability of isolated pockets.

It is fortunate that the riverine rabbit has become a flagship species for the Karoo in much the same way as the leopard has in the Cederberg. Similarly, it's now an umbrella species for conservation and rehabilitation of the region's unique riverine biomes. In the last decade, awareness of their plight has greatly increased, and conservation authorities have instituted numerous education programmes, including the Riverine-Rabbit Eco-School. The higher its profile, the better its chances of survival.

Sanbona is one of the only formally protected areas for riverine rabbits. Its size provides sufficient space and diversity for ecological processes to function naturally. It's as though a modern fairy-tale, an African version of *Watership Down*, has come to pass in which the beleaguered rabbits of the Great Karoo embarked on a final journey, an odyssey of epic proportions, over the mountains to find sanctuary in Sanbona.

In the rest of the Karoo, beyond the reserve's borders, it's up to farmers to decide whether to preserve some of their land for rabbits, or plough it under. There is proposed legislation to provide incentives for farmers to limit further development and employ conservation practices. The education of landowners and their employees is ongoing, and the creation of more private conservancies is vital to the survival of *Bunolagus monticularis*.

That evening, I went on a last game drive with Jannie. As usual, we stopped for a drink on a hill to watch the sunset. Standing there gazing at the honeyed veld, I noticed a pale object in the long grass behind Jannie. It looked like a plastic packet, or maybe a white rabbit.

"What's that?" I asked innocently.

Jannie glanced over his shoulder and said, "Oh, that's just one of our white lions."

I promptly spilt half a G&T down the front of my shirt. A white lion, here? It was the next animal on my impossible list. This was too soon. This was all wrong.

Jannie explained that Sanbona had, along with a few other South African parks, introduced white lions. So this specimen was a bred and imported cat, not the naturally occurring kind I was searching for. Phew.

The first two white lions arrived at Sanbona in 2003 as an experiment. The development of a white-lion project began in earnest with the birth of three cubs to a female named Queen. This led to the creation of a white-lion reserve—a 4,300-hectare fenced-off section of Sanbona. Eventually the offspring were integrated into a tawny-lion pride, and the reserve now boasts a self-sustaining, free-roaming pride of white and tawny lions.

"At the moment, we've got six white cats," said Jannie. "Some of the others are probably sleeping in the bushes behind that female."

I took a closer look with binoculars. She was a gorgeous specimen, snow-white with pale-blue eyes. Her pelt was slightly shaggy, like that of a polar bear. Only her snout was brown, possibly from sticking her head down a rabbit hole. She watched us with unnerving intensity. It was thrilling to be standing out in the open, face-to-face with a white lion. Fortunately the vehicle was only a few paces away and the thrill was a safe one.

It's only through human interference that the white gene can thrive. A white lion is too precious and valuable a creature to let nature decide its numbers—or so say humans. I wasn't convinced. Perhaps the handful of naturally occurring white lions that I was next to set my sights on were the only ones that really mattered. I'd have to go and see for myself.

The following morning, I loaded my bags into the vehicle. Sanbona had been a successful chapter of my quest: one-and-a-half animals had been bagged (if you counted the bred lion as a half-sighting). I bade Jannie and Keir farewell, then took the gravel track south through the mountains. As the veld spooled by, I tried to imagine a long and bounteous future for the riverine rabbit in this majestic landscape.

ASTRONAUT CATS

You can see bred white lions in any number of international zoos, as well as reserves such as Sanbona. But at the time of my initial search, there were only four known to occur naturally in the wild, and their home was the Timbavati Game Reserve in the north-eastern corner of South Africa. It was one of these extremely rare cats that I now wanted to find.

White lions are not albinos, but rather leucistic. In other words, they get their pale colouration from a recessive gene that shows up from time to time in the lion populations of the greater Kruger National Park. For a white lion to be born, both parents must carry the gene. However, the cubs seldom survive into adulthood, as they stand out like white rabbits in the veld, and are difficult to hide from predators. They are also thought to be at a disadvantage in the hunting department. Thus, adult white lions are a great rarity.

These cats were first studied back in the 1970s by a young zoologist, Chris McBride. His famous book,

The White Lions of the Timbavati, put the reserve and its cats on the map. Other reports started filtering in of white lions in the Tshokwane area of the Kruger Park, but the highest recorded prevalence of the gene is found among the Timbavati lions.

The two cubs discovered by McBride in 1975 were the first in a line of white lions that have been recorded and studied in the area. During the 1980s, McBride campaigned to have the white lions removed from the Timbavati to protect their future. This led to a situation where white lions became far more common in breeding centres, zoos, theme parks and in the nefarious canned-hunting trade, than in the wild. Today, there are probably more than three hundred white lions worldwide. They can fetch very high prices, which has led to many unethical business practices.

The Timbavati Reserve and western Kruger Park remain the only true homes of these magnificent cats, and, as some of the prides there carry the white genetic code, a new white lion can be born at any time.

My research told me the best chance of seeing one at that time was in Motswari, a small, private game reserve adjacent to the Kruger in the northern section of the Timbavati. The two most promising white lions had recently left their pride and were nomadic, ranging across vast distances, sometimes deep into the Kruger and onto private land, so getting my timing right was crucial. The Motswari team suggested that I remain on twenty-four-hour standby, and if the lions made a kill or looked settled near the lodge, I'd jump on a plane and fly to the nearest town, Hoedspruit. In theory, I could be there within hours.

In preparation for the trip, I re-read McBride's *The White Lions of Timbavati*, which I remembered from childhood. He describes how lions need their tawny camouflage to operate in the khaki-coloured world of the African veld. Their colour is all the more crucial as most prey can run faster than them, so the capacity for ambush is all-important. Being snow-white in this environment is not ideal.

McBride notes how some zoologists believe that in the past, when lions still inhabited many parts of the world, there was a greater colour variation than seen today. For instance, the lions of North Africa, which were rounded up for bloody Roman spectacles and driven to extinction, are thought to have been very pale for purposes of camouflage in the Sahara Desert.

McBride initially encountered white cubs while studying a Timbavati pride for his master's degree in wildlife management. He describes his first proper sighting in October 1975: "From a thicket emerged a tiny tawny form. Then two more furry shapes—white as polar bears, but unmistakeably lions. It was the first time I had seen them in the open... And there they all stood—Vela and the white lions of Timbavati—in the secure patch of Lowveld grass, listening as their mother called out to them."

I, too, wanted to experience a white lion emerging from the long grass to stare at me one golden Timbavati afternoon.

Weeks dragged into months, and the cats made only fleeting visits to Motswari, remaining on the move. On one occasion, the lions did hang around for a day or two, but the lodge was full and could not accommodate me. It was deeply frustrating. I imagined the white lions lounging beside the pool, sipping pink cocktails and chatting wittily to the guests while I lounged on a wretched Cape Town beach, chatting to no-one.

After a few months, the Motswari team suggested I come anyway and try my luck, as the cats kept "passing through", and there'd be no guarantees in the foreseeable future. Arriving in the Lowveld in the middle of summer, I stepped from the aircraft into a wall of heat. The veld was green and lush, with pools of standing water everywhere, allowing game and predators to roam widely with no need to find waterholes. It was an hour's drive from Hoedspruit's Eastgate Airport to Motswari through the steaming midday bush.

The lodge is traditional in look and feel: mud-coloured, thatched circular huts set among the trees beside a dry riverbed, a boma (dining stockade), and lawn with established trees around a rocky plunge pool. The camp rang with the cooing of laughing doves and shriek of cicadas. It was an Edenic spot.

Teatime was announced by the beating of drums. Guests gathered in an open-sided lounge with tree trunks poking through the thatch. Shangaan women bearing bowls on their heads arrived, singing as they laid out the food. This kind of thing always delights the tourists. Over tea and cake I met my field guide,

Shadrack Mkhabela, and his tracker, Tiyani Mashele. Shadrack was a big affable gent with a colourful use of English and the laugh of a hippo. Tiyani was a quietly spoken Shangaan, capable of tracking anything from an elephant to a dung beetle, at night, blindfolded. Both men had grown up in Mpumalanga and knew the bush intimately. Shadrack explained that as the lodge was relatively full, there would be times we'd have other guests on the 4X4, but for the most part, it would be just the three of us, and our sole objective would be to find a white lion.

The cats had not been seen in the reserve for some time, so Shadrack suggested we head to the north-eastern "Buchner" section of Motswari, bordering the Kruger, and drive the length of the boundary line to scout for spoor. The light was softening as we headed out, and the bushveld was alive with birdsong. Tiyani sat on the bonnet above the left front wheel of our open vehicle, scanning the ground for tracks.

The Timbavati, of which Motswari occupies a small part, is a five-hundred-and-fifty square kilometre chunk of Lowveld wilderness crisscrossed by sand rivers and teeming with big game. It's a primordial landscape dominated by marula, leadwood and knobthorn trees, interspersed with low acacia and grassland. Mopane, with its butterfly-shaped leaves, predominates in the north, often stunted due to the limitations of the soil. The reserve is home to more than forty species of mammal and over three-hundred-and-sixty bird species. It boasts about a hundred-and-fifty lions living in thirteen prides.

The fences between the Timbavati and Kruger have been taken down, allowing game to roam freely across vast tracts of veld.

Bone-dry through the winter months, the sandy river beds are transformed into brief torrents by the showers of summer. The veld turns from drab khaki to viridian green almost overnight. It was high summer, and the migrants had arrived in all their feathered glory: European rollers, yellow-billed kites, Diederik's cuckoos and woodland kingfishers resplendent in their incandescent turquoise livery. Ahead of us, a red-crested korhaan flew skyward as if propelled from a cannon, stalled in flight as though shot, then plummeted to the earth with his undercarriage down. It's one of the most astonishing and ludicrous mating rituals in the bush.

As we patrolled the boundary line, Shadrack filled me in on Timbavati's lions. He told me there were two white adult sisters in the Xakubasa pride, both born in May 2009. The Giraffe Farm pride had a two-year-old white lion, and the Jacaranda pride had a small white cub that was just a month old. Our best chance was going to be spotting the adult sisters. These two had led a charmed life. Most white cubs don't survive, but this pair had a powerful and protective mother and aunt to look after them. Their guardians were good teachers and successful hunters. They'd managed to kill eight giraffes during their first two months in the Motswari area, providing ample meat for the little ones. More importantly, they saw off any animal that threatened the cubs, going so far as to kill two other lions.

The Xakubasa pride was without adult males and ranged widely, covering an area of up to 40,000 hectares. The lack of stable pride males meant they needed to remain on the move, avoiding confrontation with more powerful lions. On one occasion, they were chased off a zebra kill by the three males of the Mahlathini pride, a dominant force in the region. Fleeing south, they ran into three Timbavati pride males that were also closing in on the kill. They nearly lost one of the cubs in the ensuing fight, but managed to escape and regroup. The lionesses promptly marched the cubs into the northern wilderness and didn't return for nearly a month.

"The life they are living is not an easy one," said Shadrack with admiration in his voice. "It's not a brave life, but it's a clever one. Although a mother's natural instinct is to protect her cubs, the way these lionesses guarded their young was amazing. It was almost as though they knew how special those white cubs were."

For hours we drove the eastern boundary line, trawling through open country of stunted mopane trees. It was a windless, rosy evening. However, the ground was hard from recent rain, which made for difficult tracking. Often we'd pause in a sandy river bed and get out to survey the hieroglyphics of overlapping spoor. I couldn't discern much, but Shadrack and Tiyani were able to divine a full narrative of recent traffic. Lots of everything, except lions.

We returned to the lodge after dark for a fireside dinner inside Motswari's dining stockade. The scene was a flickering fairyland of candles and hurricane lanterns.

Guests sat at tables with their field guides. Shadrack and I joined a group of Germans. The red wine flowed freely, and the warthog steaks were rare and succulent.

Shadrack told stories of his twenty-five years as a guide. "Once I was tracking lions in Sabi Sabi," he said, putting down his knife and fork as he eased into another tale. "This female came at me out of a thicket, hissing and spitting. I held my ground. She growled and I shouted at her to back off. I chambered a round in my rifle and slowly retreated. Then another lioness came charging at me from the left. She kept coming and took a flying jump. I aimed and fired!" Shadrack paused to take a sip of wine, then wiped his mouth with a big white napkin.

"The bullet tore open her head from eye to ear. She sheared away in mid-air, spraying my face and body with her blood, but she connected me a sideways blow and sent the rifle flying out of my hands. I thought she was dead. Fortunately, the other lioness backed off, still snarling. I jumped over the body, grabbed the rifle and tried to aim, but I had it the wrong way round. I was in total shock. The barrel was pointing at my chest. Just then, my partner came running and aimed his rifle at the second lioness. I screamed "No, no, no" and wrestled the gun out of his hands. She retreated.

"When we got back to the vehicle, my partner made me down a Coke and eat a sausage. As the meat touched my lips I collapsed, shaking uncontrollably. They wanted to send me to hospital, but I just stayed in bed for a few days. After that I was fine."

It transpired that the lioness wasn't dead. A team

was sent to dart her and sew up her wounds. Even her eye healed. Nevertheless, an enquiry was held into the incident. Every time a ranger or field guide shoots an animal, a thorough investigation is conducted by park authorities. Distances are measured, the position of man and beast at the time of the shooting recorded. Shadrack was completely exonerated.

Not long ago, things were quite different in the Timbavati. Shooting lions was considered sport by the locals. Shadrack recounted an incident in which a drunk farmer had gone out one night after a party to shoot a lion he'd heard roaring nearby. It had been raining heavily and his pick-up got bogged down in the mud, so he continued on foot with a torch. After walking in circles for a while, he spotted a pair of eyes in his beam and took aim, shooting the lion plumb between the eyes. The animal didn't go down. Nonplussed, he fired again. Still the animal stared back at him. The farmer ventured closer to the glowing eyes, only to discover that he hadn't missed at all. There were two bullet holes neatly placed in the grill of his pick-up.

After dinner, we gathered round the flickering embers of the bush television, glasses of Amarula in hand. Some guests held marshmallows impaled on sticks over its flames for post-dessert dessert. Conversation grew sparse, and the silences were filled with the crackling of the fire and insistent calling of a fiery-necked nightjar. It was time for bed.

Shadrack led a group of us back to the huts. Guests are not allowed to move about unaccompanied after dark as the thick riverine vegetation around camp is a favourite haunt for many large creatures, especially a group of crotchety dagga-boy buffalos. Shadrack played his torch back and forth, picking out an elephant bull destroying the tree next to reception. "I don't think he likes that acacia," said Shadrack under his breath. We gave the bull a wide berth.

Safely deposited at my hut, I brushed my teeth and got undressed. There was the snap of a branch at my front door. Puzzled, I opened it cautiously. It was pitch dark, and there was no sound other than the crickets. I stepped outside and something made me look up at the sky. Framed against the stars, a few paces away, was the enormous outline of an elephant. Another breaking branch sounded like a rifle shot and was followed by the slap of bat-wing ears against the side of his head. I stepped back into the doorway, drinking in his close proximity. What a monstrous, beautiful thing.

After a while, I climbed into bed, my ears primed for the sound of his movements around my hut, the flap of an ear, the low rumbling from his larynx. His presence filled me with an indefinable, over-brimming happiness. I dozed off thinking I didn't really need a white lion when I had an elephant next to my bed. *I had an elephant next to my bed.*

Midsummer mornings at Motswari start brutally early with a 4.30am wake-up call. We headed out into the crisp pink stillness of dawn, soon to be replaced by the white-hot remorselessness of the Lowveld day. When we passed through riparian thickets, Tiyani became festooned with spider webs, which trailed from him in long pennants of shiny gossamer. Antelope were everywhere, many with newborns. Impala babies tripped after their mothers on jerky stick legs, like Bambi ballerinas.

Shadrack was talking about the symbolism of white lions. "We have a powerful medicine man called Credo Mutwa."

"Yes, I know of him, the famous Zulu traditional healer."

"Correct. Mutwa tells us that white lions are like gods, sacred guardians of the earth. If you harm them, you harm the planet. He tells us that Timbavati means 'to come down to the ground' in the ancient Tsonga language. He says that a long time ago, before white men arrived, this place was ruled by the powerful Queen Numbi. She was very ill and close to death. Her people prayed to the ancestral spirits to send a sign that she would be saved.

"One night a big star, as bright as the sun, appeared in the sky. It was the shape of a saucer. Slowly, it descended to earth. '*Timbilé Vaa-ti!* It has come down!' shouted the people, but they were too scared to approach the strange object. A weak Queen Numbi went out to meet it, two servants supporting her. Then a creature made of light stepped out of the saucer. It held out a hand to Numbi. She said farewell to her servants and went with the creature into the saucer. That is the last they saw of her.

"For many years after that, all the animals in the area where the saucer landed gave birth to white babies. Even the lions had white cubs with blue eyes. The kings who came after Numbi declared the Timbavati a sacred place where no hunting was allowed. Although future generations of animals returned to their natural colour, still some lions continued to produce white offspring. These cats, Mutwa tells us, are children of the gods. The Bushmen had a sacred word for such a lion. They called it Tsau! It means 'star beast'. They, too, believed white lions were the children of gods." Shadrack gave one of his long, infectious chuckles.

"Do you believe it?" I asked.

"No, no, for me it's just good stories."

We decided to check the south-eastern border next to the Kruger. After a few fruitless hours searching for spoor, we stopped for coffee. Shadrack laid a table with nibbles, rusks and silverware. Just then two armed men stepped from the bush, their LM5 semi-automatic rifles unslung. "Uh-oh," I thought, looking around for the nearest termite mound to dive behind.

However, their smiles suggested we weren't about to be pumped full of holes. They were members of a SANParks unit hunting the poachers responsible for killing the Kruger's rhinos. Tiyani made them each a mug of hot chocolate. They spoke in Shangaan, and Shadrack translated for my benefit. The men told us they walked up to fifty kilometres a day. If they came across human tracks, they followed them until they found the poacher, even if it took days and led them far outside the park. The two young men were fit, strong and dedicated. They were on the frontline in the fight to save South Africa's rhinos from the voracious Asian market.

Shadrack asked about white lions, and the men said

there was an elephant kill close by that might be promising. But it was on the Kruger side of the boundary, and we weren't allowed to cross. A line of vultures, etched against the dark-blue sky, headed towards the carcass. We were on the western edge of a vast expanse of pure wilderness in a trackless corner of the Kruger. A white lion could be born, live a full life, and die there—and no-one would be the wiser. There was something tremendously comforting in such knowledge.

Driving back to camp, Shadrack was again speaking about Mutwa's strange theories. "The sangoma tells us that white lions show evidence of having been snow animals."

"You've got to be joking," I said.

"Seriously. He says the thick mane and paw formations were adapted for glacial conditions. The old man says the khaki-coloured bushveld is not a good environment for a snow-white lion. He says that only under extreme conditions would a white mutation be favoured. He thinks such conditions would have occurred during an Ice Age."

"So these snow lions are both Ice Age mutants *and* offspring of star gods?"

"That's what he tells us." Shadrack winked at me, then burst out laughing. He was damn good company on an otherwise dull game outing.

We'd set off on long drives each morning and evening, usually tracing Motswari's perimeters to look for incoming lion tracks. Shadrack put out regular radio calls to other vehicles in the Timbavati, asking about any sign of *ngala yakubasa*—white lion. The answers remained negative. However, we were repeatedly, and pleasantly, distracted from our quest by excellent sightings of other large game. The objective of my Impossible Five quest was the very opposite of Big Five hunting, but if such creatures kept presenting themselves on a platter, there was no harm in looking. Take, for instance, the elephant bull with some of the biggest tusks any of us had ever seen, which sauntered up to our vehicle, stuck its trunk in and had a good sniff at its occupants. We sat absolutely still, terrified and excited. Or the white rhino that ran off at our approach, one of its hind legs showing a deep incision where a poacher's snare had cut into the flesh. I was glad to see its skittishness, as it sported a magnificent pair of horns.

We saw large herds of buffalo and, on one occasion, came to a waterhole where a cow had just given birth. The glistening calf was trying to stand on Plasticine legs while its mother and a group of females stood in a circle offering encouragement.

Nearby, a bull danced about in a state of what looked like euphoria. Perhaps he was the father celebrating the birth of his child. The animal leaped about, then rolled on his back in the water, flicking mud into the air with his horns like a juggler. He charged in circles, bucking, kicking out his hind legs and head-butting the air as though practicing for a matador encounter. It was an astonishing display. The rest of the herd stood about chewing the cud with indulgent expressions that clearly said, "proud dad having his moment", while he went on bellowing, "Oh joy, oh new life!"

One late afternoon, a call came through on the radio saying an *ingwe* had been seen close to camp. I hadn't really managed to spot a Cape leopard, so I wasn't going to miss out on the (admittedly more common) Lowveld variety. "Let's pause on the white cats for a bit and go see a spotted one," I suggested.

Shadrack needed no encouraging. He slammed the Land Rover into reverse, spun us through a three-point turn and headed off at high speed. We were a long way from the sighting, and the leopard was mobile. Insects whirred by, low branches required us to duck, and Tiyani nearly came unstuck from his bonnet seat through the turns as we closed rapidly on our quarry.

"She's *fambad* (Shangaan for vamoosed) into riverine thicket; we've lost her," said the voice on the radio.

This didn't deter Shadrack, and within fifteen minutes we reached the spot. I could hear the other vehicle searching the riverbed to our right, but couldn't see it in the dense vegetation.

If the leopard had gone to ground, there was no way we could follow her into such thick undergrowth. It was already dusk and we were fast losing light. I felt the sinking leopard feeling I knew so well from the Cederberg.

Just then, a spotted cat stepped through the leaves twenty metres ahead of us. She stopped and stared at the vehicle. I held my breath. Shadrack cut the engine. For an eternity that was probably a handful of seconds, our eyes locked. Two yellow orbs bored into me. The hairs on the back of my neck stood respectfully to attention.

She moved off, striding through the long grass with a regal swagger, hips rolling, head hung low. Shadrack bundu-bashed to keep up, snapping branches and upending bushes in the process. The leopard paused beside a fallen tree, rubbed her head and body against the trunk, scent-marked the bark, then pressed on into the dusk, her colouration blending perfectly with the leafy vegetation. Dapples on dapples, spots on spots. She was all menace and grace and fearful symmetry.

Shadrack manoeuvred the vehicle around a clump of trees and positioned it directly in her path. Undeterred, she kept coming, straight at us. Closer and closer, until she was alongside, now brushing our back tyre with her shoulder as she passed within arm's length. Tiyani shifted slightly in his seat, and she bared her fangs with a low hiss. If I'd been in Tiyani's position, I would have been quivering like blancmange.

In the distance, an impala let out a sharp alarm call, and a herd took off as though a gun had been fired, their graceful bodies winging through the darkening trees. By now it was almost night, and both vehicles trained spotlights on the cat. She slipped into a thicket and emerged with a young impala in her mouth. The antelope's delicate head lolled in her jaws as if asleep: a lover in a final embrace. The blood of its flayed torso glowed scarlet in the beam of our spot.

"We're gonna have to lock this down, everyone," said Shadrack into the microphone. "The *ingwe* has a kill. Let's leave her to enjoy the meal. Over and out."

He explained to me that with so many hyenas in the

vicinity, spotlights would reveal that she had a kill, and the meal could easily be stolen from her. He turned the vehicle round and slowly bundu-bashed towards the road. I looked back and saw a vague shape slink into the undergrowth: the princess of darkness with her dinner.

Timbavati offered plenty of good sightings to keep me distracted from the paucity of lions: a vocal pod of hippos at our sundowner spot, a hyena den with cheeky pups, and three giant eagle owls in a row. We were treated to a bushbaby jousting with a puffadder, and many a warm, star-filled night thronged with nightjars and echoing with the yelp of jackals. Once we stopped to watch the hilarious antics of a dwarf-mongoose manor. They poked their puppet heads from myriad holes, all industry and inquisitiveness, darting in and out as if on Ritalin.

Most of the time I was alone on the vehicle with Shadrack and Tiyani, and we could concentrate on white-lion hunting. When the lodge filled up and our vehicle could no longer be spared, we were joined by guests, often fresh off the plane from strange, foreign-sounding places like London and Berlin. On such occasions, we had to tick off all the essentials, especially the Big Five, while still covertly searching for pale lions. Every squirrel and every impala needed to be photographed. Flying bananas (yellow-billed hornbills) and flying chillies (red-billed hornbills) were fussed and cooed over as though they were rare exotics.

Actually, it was rather fun having company on the vehicle, and the observations and enthusiasm of bushveld newbies were always entertaining. Sightings came quickly, some of them called in on the radio, others found by vulture-eyed Tiyani. It being December and with Christmas fast approaching, the encounters took on the characteristics of a carol: "On the twelfth day of Christmas, my ranger gave to me... twelve hippos honking, eleven jackals howling, ten frogs-a-jumping, nine whydahs dancing, eight leopards leaping, seven crocs-a-swimming, six Egyptian geese-a-laying, five golden lions, four go-away birds, three moor hens, two turtle doves and a coucal in a thorn tree."

Some guests were nervous of the bush and offered the occasional, high-pitched "back up, driver!" when elephants came too close. Others were disconcerted by the amount of insect life during night drives. Attracted by the lights, winged creatures would make a beeline for the open vehicle. There'd be the odd squawk of alarm as something large and droning whizzed by. Approaching dung beetles sounded like Huey helicopters on a strafing run. One evening, a portly German took a beetle on his forehead with the sound of a decently struck cricket ball. Both vehicle and insect were doing about thirty kilometres per hour, so the impact was considerable. "Ha, ha, you all zink it's zo very funny," said the victim sarcastically, the deathly silence belying our collective mirth. To be honest, we did zink zo.

Not finding white lions was proving extremely pleasant. I didn't mind if the waiting dragged on for weeks, even months. A comfortable hut on a leafy bend of the Sohobele River, a plunge pool for dips, tasty meals and a daily procession of game moving through our unfenced camp: what more could one ask for? As I sat outdoors with my laptop, an elephant snacked on a nearby tree, then sucked up a trunk full of sand and tossed clouds of the red earth over its head, like talcum powder. A large-spotted genet snoozed on a mopane branch directly above my head. I watched as the creature adjusted itself in its sleep, a sinuous body and long furry tail wedged in a fork of the tree. If it had a nightmare or rolled over carelessly in its sleep, there might have been a nasty mid-air awakening, and a grumpy cat on my laptop.

The heat would grow more intense through the day, enforcing frequent swims. Thunderheads built up, and with them the pressure. After lunch would come the rumble of celestial artillery from the Drakensberg escarpment, which stood like a battlement on the western horizon. It was an elemental and godly tableau.

Our bend in the river was a noisy one. Between the trilling of Cape turtle doves, squabbling of arrow-mark babblers, glugging of green-spotted doves and shriek of cicadas, you could hardly get a word in edgeways. The sound had a soporific effect, and, combined with the heat, often made writing or even reading impossible as eyelids drooped and arms were overcome by an unbearable floppiness.

A lazy mosquito, its propellers only just keeping it aloft, droned past my ear. A lizard with an iridescent blue tail basked on a rock beside me. A paradise flycatcher landed on a twig, his blue eyes watching my fingers on the keyboard, his orange tail twitching. He was a Chinese dancer trailing ribbons ten times the length of his body.

A warm breeze disturbed the shiny undersides of the mopane leaves, creating a disco effect. Another swim, perhaps. Or was it siesta time again? Such exhausting decisions.

I knew I couldn't keep taking advantage of Motswari hospitality forever. So, one afternoon I made the terrible decision to log onto the internet and book an SA Express flight out of Hoedspruit for the following day. Over dinner, I told Shadrack it was now his sacred duty to find me a white lion the next morning, even if he had to dart and Tippex a tawny one in the night. "I'll see what I can do," he said. Which sounded vaguely promising.

I woke in the early hours to the roaring of a lion in the distance. Was Shadrack working his magic? It's one of those sounds that really gets your attention: a reminder of which predator is king of the bush. I imagined a big male standing out in the open, the sound coming from deep inside his chest, a gruff, explosive rumble, followed by a series of guttural grunts.

We set off at first light. Shadrack and Tiyani had also heard the roaring in the night, and we headed in that general direction. It was a still, luminous dawn, cool and magical, with tendrils of mist lingering among the trees. Impala and wildebeest shook themselves into wakefulness; littl'uns gambolled about joyfully. A startled Swainson's spurfowl scurried away from our tyres, emitting a raucous cackle. We trawled the northern access road towards Buchner, from where the roaring had emanated. Back and forth we went. Hours passed. The day grew steamy.

Our spirits flagged. I began clock-watching, as I needed to be at the airport by noon.

Shadrack allowed the vehicle to glide to a halt without touching the brake and switched off the engine. "They're not exactly white, but they're probably in the process of making a white one," he said in a stage whisper. About twenty metres to our left lay a pair of lions taking a break between bouts of mating.

"They're from the Mahlatini pride," said Shadrack under his breath. "Both carry the white gene. As you can see, she's very pale and he has a small, underdeveloped mane—both signs of the gene."

The male looked regal and possessive, watching his paramour's every move. He presented a magnificent sight with blow-dried blond hair and neatly trimmed goatie. When the lioness was ready to resume, she stood up, sauntered over and rubbed her body against his snout. He needed no second invitation. She crouched and he stood over her, baring his teeth and letting out a strange sound like an ibis learning to play the trumpet underwater. It was over in seconds. As he dismounted, she took a swipe at him with a saucepan paw. He jumped back to avoid the blow. Then she rolled onto her back, a pure white belly pointing at the sky. He came and lay next to her, watching intently for a sign to initiate the next round. "They'll carry on like this all day," whispered Shadrack. "Lions can mate up to fifty times in a session."

If their coupling was successful, a litter would be born in three months. One of the cubs might well be white. This union between two cats carrying the white gene was the closest I was going to get to Timbavati's white lions, those mythical star beasts bequeathed to us by a flying saucer.

And I had an SA Express saucer to catch.

Two years passed and the white lions had nagged at the back of my mind all the while. Both the Cederberg's spotted cats and the Lowveld's white cats had eluded me. I remained in touch with my contacts in the Timbavati, and they told me of occasional sightings. In the meantime, I'd begun reading about Linda Tucker's Global White Lion Trust. This intrepid former model and Cambridge graduate had created a private reserve on the border of the Timbavati where she has released white lions back into the wild.

As luck would have it, I was offered an assignment to write an article about lodges in the western Kruger for an in-flight magazine. I arranged to add a couple of extra days to the trip so that I could meet Linda. It would be my best shot at seeing a wild white lion on its home range.

I'd heard a lot about Linda, both in the press and through family connections, but my reading only posed more questions than answers. I discovered that she's a passionate conservationist with total commitment to her cause of saving white lions. The trust she'd set up saw to the protection of these rare cats and developing the cultural values that hold them sacred in many traditional societies, but she was also into some fairly esoteric shamanistic stuff, which was both intriguing and confounding.

Reading Linda's two books, *Mystery of the White Lions* and *Saving the White Lions*, I learnt about the Damascus moment in her life. It involved a brush with death that took place in November 1991. She was on an evening game drive with a safari group in a remote part of the Timbavati when their 4X4 hit a tree stump that broke the steering column. The group was stranded in the middle of the bush with a non-functioning radio. A pride of lions started to pay them unwanted attention, and soon surrounded the vehicle. The guests were petrified. One tourist started screaming, which prompted snarls and growls from the cats.

Just then, a woman appeared out of the darkness, walking towards them without a torch. She was dressed in tribal gear with a baby on her back and two children in tow. Seemingly in a trance, she walked between the lions, which stopped growling and immediately calmed down. She'd miraculously come to their rescue, pacifying the lions and allowing the ranger to walk through the pride and back to the lodge to fetch a second vehicle.

Up until then, Linda had been a high-flying model and marketing consultant in London, Paris and New York. But this moment was to transform her life. It took Linda three years to extricate herself from her European existence and return to Africa in search of the woman who'd saved them.

Maria Khosa, also known as the Lion Queen of Timbavati, revealed to Linda her "sacred destiny": to become the Keeper of the White Lions. Maria hailed from a lineage of lion shamans, and was to teach Linda all she knew about the ancient lore and spiritual weaponry needed for the task ahead.

As Shadrack had told me, oral records recount that white lions appeared four centuries ago during the reign of Queen Numbi, when a meteoritic event of some kind occurred in the Timbavati region. Linda came to understand that white lions were the holiest animals in Africa, and that to harm one was to harm the land; to kill one was to kill the soul of Africa. She realised that by committing herself to the conservation of these cats, she would assist in the protection of other kingdoms and eco-systems, and could be of service to a higher cause, making a meaningful contribution to humanity. Or so her books suggested.

Credo Mutwa contends that white lions originate from the star Sirius and the Orion constellation, known as Matsieng. These cats are "guardians of the human soul and invite us to re-awaken our own souls in order to protect the planet." Through his teachings, Linda learnt of the urgency of the cause. White lions appear on Earth as prophets in periods of crisis. They are said to hold the key to saving humanity in this time of ecological disaster.

Khosa prophesied that in the near future, on a day of great significance, a new queen of the white lions would be born. Linda would be this cat's protector. And so it came to pass. On 25 December 2000, in the Free State town of Bethlehem, a snowy-white lion was born. From the moment Linda took little Marah in her arms, she knew she would dedicate her life to freeing this queen and her family from the trophy hunters who held her captive. It became Linda's mission to return Marah, and future white lions, to the land of their birthright.

To do this, she needed funding. Lots of it. Linda established her Global Trust: its first objective was to secure Marah's freedom and then release her onto a piece of land in the Timbavati region. She teamed up with Jason Turner, a lion ecologist who'd spent years studying the Timbavati prides. He became her business partner, scientific adviser and lover.

With the help of generous donor funding from around the globe, Marah was rescued from the hunters and a farm that was to become known as Tsau was purchased. Despite numerous attempts by local hunters to stop her, Linda's dream became reality in 2005. Marah and her cubs would be the progenitors of generations of white lions born on their ancestral soil.

At the conclusion of my Kruger assignment, I was dropped at Eastgate Airport to await a transfer to Linda's ranch. I was collected in a pick-up by Lee, one of the staff at Tsau. She was a tall blond woman who'd worked in marketing in London for fifteen years. She'd recently returned to South Africa and joined the white-lion team. As we drove, Lee told me about the Trust and about Linda. "She's an incredible woman. Powerful, intelligent, strong. She carries this whole project on her shoulders." Lee's tone was reverential, like that of an acolyte.

"My uncle and Linda's mother were friends," I said.

Lee looked surprised: "Oh, Linda never talks about

her past. She's so focused on the task at hand."

"From what I've read, she's made a lot of enemies in the Lowveld."

"Yes, but Linda's a fighter, and she has total faith in her lions."

We arrived at the main gate, where Lee used telemetry to make sure there were no lions nearby before getting out to open it. A short drive through the bush brought us to Unicorn Camp, where she showed me to my hut. I was to make myself comfortable; Linda would join me later.

The hut was hobgoblin in shape, with a dormer window in the thatch and a web of beams in place of a ceiling. It was decorated with antique furniture and kelims, paraffin lamps and Ndebele dolls; the base of an old Singer sewing machine served as a table. Wasps droned in and out through open windows. Above two single beds were artworks by Linda's mother, Margaret Maskew: an etching of a boy and a sketch of a woman carrying wood.

I took a stroll around camp. There wasn't anyone about. Huts were decorated in geometric patterns of dots and wave patterns. There was a large hammock, a small plunge pool and a number of striking sculptures, many of them Henry Miller-inspired torsos or statues with sun or moon heads. The open-sided lodge was divided into dining- and living-room sections with a fire pit in between. The thatched roofs were supported by leadwood tree trunks. It was all tastefully done, more homely than the usual safari-lodge style.

Images of white lions hung on the walls. Scattered

about were items used in rituals: drums, a reindeer antler, masks from across the African continent. On a table beneath a big photograph of a white lion stood a shrine of sorts. There were effigies of white and winged lions, a few sphinxes, a white horse and a map of Africa with a row of gold and quartzite pyramids running down its length. The pale-blue eyes of the lion stared down at me. I was starting to feel a little uncomfortable. What, exactly, was I letting myself in for?

I came to a circular stockade and stepped inside. The reed enclosure had a concrete floor and central fire pit. To the right stood a big white lion made from wire and beads. I knew that !Xam, Inuit, Ndebele and other elders and shamans visited Tsau to celebrate equinoxes and the like. Around the stockade's perimeter lay a range of items left over from various ceremonies. There were kudu horns, Buddhist religious items, the remains of candles and pieces of wood in the shape of human torsos. Among the charred logs of the fire pit, I noticed beaded dolls and the shells of giant African land snails.

To be honest, I was starting to get a spooky feeling. I knew Linda wasn't running a cult or anything of that ilk, but I had a nagging suspicion that I might be biting off more than I could chew. And I was slightly nervous about meeting "the white-lion woman". The heat was oppressive and thunderheads built overhead, adding to the pressure. All the while, the call of a crested barbet was drilling a hole in my head with its infernal "ke-ke-ke-ke".

Walking back to my room, I glanced left to see a white creature bounding towards me. I'd viewed enough white-lion images in the previous half hour to have a fairly strong impression that I was about to be felled by one of Linda's cats. Having leapt half out of my skin, I realised it was a Labrador, and an amiable one at that. I wondered how many foreign guests had had the wits scared out of them by Maxi's exuberant greetings.

Just then, Linda, tall, gorgeous, with blond hair showing dark at the roots, appeared round the side of a building. "Justin!" she said. "How come it's taken so long?"

"I haven't the foggiest. Wonderful to meet you!"

"It's such a hot day, let's sit with our feet in the pool and have a chat." She had a broad smile and sonorous voice. Her eyes were brown, a string of beads was wrapped around her wrist, and two white lions, back to back, adorned a necklace at her throat.

We took off our shoes and socks and sat side-by-side. Both of us were anxious, it seemed. I carried so much expectation, and, from what I'd heard, she was wary of journalists or visitors who sought to represent, or misrepresent, her project.

"You've come such a long way to see our lions," she said. Her voice was compelling, demanding my full attention.

I explained my impossible-five quest and told her that white lions were my last port of call. She gave me a brief outline of their work at Tsau. Then conversation turned to our families. Her mother and my uncle, the Afrikaner poet Uys Krige, had been best friends in the 1970s and 1980s. In fact, Linda's mother, whom I remembered well from childhood visits, had written a book about my uncle, *A Portrait of Uys Krige*. Linda went inside and returned with a gift copy for me.

"My mom always described Margaret as an angel," I said. "You have her smile."

"Thank you," she said, beaming.

Linda and I had gone to brother-and-sister schools and been undergraduates at the same university. I'd visited her home as a child, and she mine, but we'd never met before. Any thoughts I might have had of poking fun at Linda's white-lion obsession were fast evaporating.

She spoke about acquiring Tsau. "When I came here the first time, I found a rocky promontory that looked as though it had been lifted straight from *The Lion King*. If you remember, in the movie all the animals of the savannah gather to pay homage to the newborn royal cub, who stands on Pride Rock with his parents, surveying the kingdom. I imagined Marah doing that one day with her cubs." Her eyes shone. It was hard to resist being drawn in.

"On the afternoon we released Marah into the wild, I was able to hold her while she was still drugged. Her fresh, cut-hay scent, her warm, soft flank. If I'd been granted one wish, I would have shape-shifted and become a lioness there and then. I thought of Marah as my daughter. I have never known any love so strong."

Linda talked about the tragedy of canned-lion hunting in South Africa, and the need for tight security at Tsau. "Poachers, professional hunters and aggressive neighbours are always a threat. Jason has set up an armed-response unit and I use shamanic techniques to create an invisible force field around our perimeter. The energy shield forms a pyramid of pure light and even renders our lions invisible from the air."

I thought of suggesting that the military might be interested in her energy shield, but held my tongue. Linda told me that there were only a few thousand lions left in the wild, but more than double that number in captivity, many of them bred for the trophy-hunting industry. Of the former, only about a dozen are white. "You go to these petting farms where you can play with cute little lion cubs, but when they grow bigger they're kept in cages until they are ready to be shot," she said. "The whole sordid business has become industrialised. And being so rare, white lions are the most sought after."

We put on our shoes and walked to the open Land Cruiser, where I met her partner, the lion ecologist Jason Turner. He was a tall, handsome fellow with spectacles and a gentle air. Jason had done his master's studies in the Timbavati, where he'd examined the predation patterns of local prides. His research was ongoing, and he was comparing the hunting patterns of white and tawny lions. He was about to publish a paper showing, contrary to those who believed that white lions had a big camouflage disadvantage, that there was no difference between them and the tawnies. In fact, on full-moon nights, white lions appeared to have a slightly better kill rate than their khaki-coloured cousins.

"We've introduced tawny lions from the Kalahari into our prides. They have strong genes, they're resilient and don't have TB or feline Aids, which is rife among Kruger cats and disastrous for conservation." He stopped the vehicle and raised a telemetry aerial above his head. "I have a good signal from one of our Kalahari lionesses right now. She's really, really close, but I can't seem to spot her."

"Pulling a disappearing act again," muttered Linda.

"There she is!" I exclaimed.

"Where?" they both chimed.

"Look up."

"Good grief!" said Linda.

The lioness was balancing on top of a dam wall.

"A flying lion!" exclaimed Linda. "She's never done that before. Must have known you were coming."

"Cat on a hot tin roof," I said.

"Her name is Tswalu," said Jason. "She's from the Oppenheimers' Kalahari reserve, such a pretty lady. She's been mating with our two white males. We'll try to find them for you before the light goes."

Low clouds had rolled in, and the air was stifling. The occasional thunderous rumble intensified the atmosphere. I was feeling anxious again. Finally, after more than two years, I was going to see the last of my darling, infernal impossibles.

We drove on. The light dimmed. The cumulonimbus clouds almost touched the treetops. I was all a-jitter.

"Over there!" said Jason.

The two snow-white lads were lying in the road, sound asleep. We sidled up and parked within ten metres of the beauties. And, oh my goodness, they were beautiful. I was transfixed.

"These are Zukhara and Matsieng," said Linda. "The latter is a name created by Credo Mutwa and means 'Orion' or 'Hercules' in Zulu. These are the grandsons of Marah, the first two to be born on our land and fully integrated into the environment."

Linda stared intently at the lions. One of them gazed back at her with inquisitive eyes. I'd read that Linda contended she could enter a realm shamans call "dreamtime", where she met the lions on their own terms and spoke "the language of souls".

"I know you've just arrived and this might still be a bit weird for you, but... would you like to join me in meditation?" asked Linda. Her question seemed a sensual invitation to some sort of transition, transgression even. An introduction, perhaps, to a secret world. I must confess that I had the odd goosebump.

"Um, okay," I said.

"We need to circumvent your rational mind and get into your deeper consciousness. Let's see what comes, even if it's only a profound sense of peace. Close your eyes and slow your breathing. Be completely relaxed. As you breathe in, be aware of the gift that nature gives us, the oxygen of life that we breathe in from the trees. Visualise that your body's system has trees—the branches and capillaries of your lungs. Draw that breath into the furthest parts of your body, right into your cells.

"As you breathe in, take the flame of life into your body. Let it burn away anything that holds you back. Breathe in light and breathe out darkness. In with light, out with disease. You are part of the great cycle of life. Regenerate your system with light. Lions symbolise this light. Let out any fear, resentment, anger, any confusion. Let it out!" It was a hissed exhortation.

"Let yourself be restored by the cosmos that has love as its source. Breathe in the light of the eco-system, of the sun. Now your body is vibrating with the frequency of sunlight, the pure gold of creation. Breathe in light and breathe out light."

I opened my eyes a crack and saw how keenly one of the lions was watching Linda. He seemed mesmerised. I was close enough to smell her perfume. Her unruly mane of hair was centimetres from my face, tugged by the breeze. The experience was sensuous, unsettling.

"Now you *are* light," she whispered. "Start to expand your consciousness. You're creating light around you. It dissolves anything in your world that is not of the light. You are one with your environment, rippling out pure light across the land. Allow this light to expand, dissolving all human-made objects. Become one with the sun's light and with love. You are the light of creation. Shine your light!"

I had pins and needles in one of my legs, but didn't want Linda to think I wasn't rapt, so I quietly straightened it, feeling the prickly rush. Relief. I stole a glance at the cat beside the vehicle, his enormous muscular body, the nodes of his spine, the veins in his back, a shaggy mane matted with thorns and twigs. And those eerily blue eyes.

"Allow the lions to give you a message," murmured

Linda. "Open your heart. Don't doubt! Don't question!"

There was silence. She resumed her deep breathing. I copied her.

A rustling of clothes suggested proceedings had come to a close. I opened my eyes. The lions yawned, exposing pink gums and long canines. They stretched luxuriantly, stood up and sauntered off. Had they been waiting for Linda to finish? Had they also been meditating? I was caught in a web of sceptical, topsy-turvy awe. Damn, perhaps she had something.

"Did the lions give you a message?" she asked.

I'd heard the wind, the swishing grass and the birds, but not a peep from the lions.

"No, I'm sorry. I just felt very peaceful."

"That's okay, maybe next time," she said, sounding disappointed. Perhaps I hadn't been on the same frequency. I thought I'd make a joke about checking my email to see if there was a message from the lads, but desisted.

The lions swaggered down the white sand road into the darkening west. Lighting split the horizon. The pair glowed like the star beasts Linda believed they were, and who was I to argue? Grey ghosts, ethereal beings of the Timbavati twilight. With their fabulous hairdos and carrot-up-the-bum gaits, they looked for all the world like Benny and Bjorn from Abba. Dancing queens both.

"The sort of meditation you've just experienced is the early stage of the kind of thing I do in my leadership workshops," said Linda. "Telepathy functions on the love vibration. We feel a real connection with these lions, with their solar energy. Even their faces look like the sun and the manes are the rays, don't you think?"

Yes, but I didn't really know what I was thinking. In fact, thinking was becoming extremely difficult. So I stopped.

Back at the lodge, Jason opened a bottle of Diemersdal Sauvignon Blanc. "We don't normally serve wine at Tsau," said Linda. "It dulls the senses when you're working with lions. But let's make an exception tonight, shall we?"

We sat at a long table. Linda was all star beasts and mythology. Jason was all science and logic. They kept looking at each other for validation as they spoke. To my ear, they seemed to be talking parallel languages. However, there was no doubt they made an excellent team. It was exhilarating to be in their company.

Jason laid out the facts: "The hunting practices around here are all wrong. Hunters always want the dominant males, but these carry the best genes. Taking them out also creates massive disruption among the prides. I'd estimate that there are more than two-hundred unethical farmers producing lions for hunting or for sale. There's so much inbreeding that these cats are degenerate, and they're also imprinted by humans, making their release into the wild impossible."

"Between Tsau and our two other parcels of land we have seven white lions," said Linda. "Ultimately we would love to drop the fences on at least one boundary, but obviously not with Timbavati, which allows trophy-hunting. As more white cubs are born, there will be an increasing need for land."

"What we really need is to change the hunting mind-set in America," Jason cut in. "The US accounts for more than sixty percent of trophy-hunting in South Africa. Local game farmers always crow about the huge revenue foreign hunters bring into the country, but it's an infinitesimal fraction of GDP. In any case, it's been proved that photographic safaris generate more revenue than hunting. Lions in Africa are progressively losing out to humans. They've had eighty percent of their original home ranges taken away. Unfortunately, our government is closely advised by the hunting fraternity."

"What is positive, though, is the international outcry," said Linda. "The global march for lions is a case in point. The power of social media is incredible. We had nearly one-and-a-half million signatures. It started in Cape Town, but by the time we finished, sixty-two cities around the world had taken part. A billboard was put up in Joburg outside the airport showing President Jacob Zuma with a gun to the head of a lion. There was a court case demanding that it be removed, but the lion advocates won."

Roast chicken was served in a casserole dish. Linda suggested we hold hands. I assumed we were about to say grace, but I was mistaken. "We have so many religions and nationalities among our guests that we simply offer a moment of silence," she said. "We use this opportunity to say our own prayers for nature and ask forgiveness from the chicken we are about to consume."

Jason took my hand in one of his big paws. Linda

took my other hand, her thumb running gently over my knuckles. There was perhaps too much intimacy, even if a chicken had lost its life in the creation of this dinner. I'd only just met these two humans. It felt as though we were about to commit a crime. I closed my eyes and tried to think of the chicken, but could only picture a battery farm and a thousand birds in a line of cages. After a while, Linda squeezed my hand again, perhaps to indicate that the chicken was satisfied, and began to carve.

Jason had been leading genetic research on white lions with a team from seven countries. He explained how they had compared the genetics of snow leopard, tiger, snow bear and white lion. They'd finally cracked the genetic code for white lions—a coup that had recently been announced on the BBC and in *Nature* magazine.

"We needed the code to make the case to have them proclaimed a protected subspecies or variant unique to a region. The snow bear of British Columbia has been declared a subspecies of *Ursus americanus*," he explained.

"Canadian indigenous nations have prophesies about white bears that are similar to the ones we have with white lions," said Linda. "They say that these 'spirit bears' are associated with the creation moment on Earth."

Jason interjected, "What's important is that the whole subpopulation of black bears in the region are then protected, because they are carrying the white gene. This is the model we need to use for our white lions. We want them to be the capstone species of the whole biosphere. If we can get them protected, then all tawny lions in the region would also need to be protected, as they could be carrying the gene."

"Modern humans have lost so much of their instinctive potential," said Linda, changing tack. "Part of the gift of my training with Maria Khosa was how she opened me up to many other levels of interface with nature. It was no longer an 'us-them' approach that objectified nature. She belonged to an ancient lineage of lion priestesses who could cross the species barrier. They did so through ceremony and a condition of reverence for divinity in nature.

"At certain times of year, for example during the harvest, lion priestesses would make an offering to the dominant male of a pride and place ceremonial beer at a sacred site. When the lions made their next kill, the priestess would walk into the pride and be allowed to carve off a piece of meat, which she would then take back to her people. Such practices were outlawed by the Timbavati authorities, who called it 'carcass robbing'. In my research, I've come across accounts by early European explorers in Africa that mention this very practice.

"Part of the training we do in my White Lion Leadership Academy is to draw on ancient knowledge, combine it with modern science and bring it into play in our current crisis. The objective is to inspire and empower participants to embody white-lion leadership principles, improve their own intellectual, emotional and physical wellbeing, and also the wellbeing of our planet.

"So the meditation technique I did with you helps you transcend your ego consciousness. You get beyond that buzz of instant gratification and constant need for technological distraction. You need to access the flow of love that exists between all species, even the apex predator and humans. You dissolve physical borders and start to merge with the auric field of the lions. These cats have a large field of energy around them, part of their healing ability. It's a vibration of light." She smiled wryly. "One has to be very careful of how you talk about this so that it doesn't sound... weird.

"A lot of wisdom comes through this process of merging. You're able to release all sorts of inhibitions and disease held in your body. For instance, we know that dolphins have the ability to cure. All animals have different ways of restoring and healing. Lions work with the frequency of sunlight. White lions are sunlight incarnate."

Linda talked deep into the night about her snowy lions and the mythology that surrounded them. Ancestral sources held that the Sphinx of Egypt and Timbavati were both on the "prime meridian", which corresponds with the Rift Valley and a subterranean seam of gold running down the length of Africa, holding Earth's axis in place. At a level of prophesy, returning the white lions to their sacred lands meant they would once again perform their role as protectors of Earth's axis.

"The Egyptians called this meridian the line of first time. The Sphinx was of course a lion, guarding the golden meridian, and lions were associated with the stars, especially the Leo constellation. The lion represents order, balance, harmony and justice on Earth, and you'll find its symbolism everywhere: Trafalgar Square, St

Mark's Square in Venice, the symbols used by banks and governments, so much of Christian imagery. I believe it's not just symbolism, but reality. The white lion returns to Earth to bring about peace and harmony with nature, restoring cosmic order."

"But Linda," I said. "So much of what you say requires such a giant leap of faith."

"You know, Jason—"

"I'm Justin, that's Jason on your right."

She smiled indulgently. "You know, *Justin*, I've observed how the fiercely rational arguments go round and round in circles, but miss the mark entirely. The key to understanding is to open your heart. Intellectualising won't get you there. Trust your instincts, believe in your dreams."

Later, I sat outside my hut, looking at the stars and thinking about Linda. Like W.B. Yeats, she had created a personal mythology that borrowed from many sources. There was Jung and shamanism, astrology and ancient symbolism, First Nation lore and African mysticism all rolled into a belief system that sort of made sense if you suspended your disbelief from a very high branch. She used her intellect and debating skills to make her case, and had amassed a wealth of data to support her ideas. However, if she brought Jason's scientific logic to bear on her theories, many of them would collapse. And yet, it did seem as though she'd telepathically communicated with the lions. I'd seen the way Matsieng's big blue eyes had locked onto her big brown eyes. There was certainly something going on there.

Linda had said that these "children of the sun god"

brought a message of light and harmony. Would humans keep fighting, trying to hold onto their egotistical position of control and domination of Earth, thereby destroying everything? Although the sceptic in me could not go along with the spiritual dimension of her thesis, I did recognise a powerful metaphor. My impossible-five quest was, in this sense, an assertion of wilderness, an avowal of the rights of wild animals, and a celebration of the elusive ones that remained unspotted, even as humans gobbled up the land all around them in the name of progress.

Linda said that our species had broken its contract with nature: taking without giving back, receiving without thanking, consuming with such greed that we've all but destroyed the fabric of love that connects all things on our planet. Once we remembered the love bond that exists between all things, we'd be on the path to reclaiming our own souls. I wasn't sure about my soul, but the idea of love made sense. A reverence for nature. In my mind, the five impossibles were recast as my personal apex animals, capstone species that could represent all of nature for me, from lowly worm to lofty elephant. This I could learn from Linda.

It was an early start the next morning. The three of us would be joined by three young interns volunteering at Tsau. I met Linda for a cup of coffee at the fire pit, where the remains of the previous evening's logs were still smoking. She was dressed in khaki, a matching amber necklace and earrings, and wore her hair scraped back in a bun. Despite the ungodly hour, she looked ravishing.

The young women arrived and we set off in the open vehicle. Jason soon found the two white lions, fast asleep after a night spent patrolling the borders of their territory. This time, we would do a group meditation. Linda spoke to the volunteers: "Today, you need to try to merge with the auric field of the lions. As a group, we can enhance that field. Let us begin."

While the others slowed their breathing and drifted into dreamy states, I watched Linda and her cats. We went through the same ritual as the previous evening. My stomach grumbled so loudly I thought it might be mistaken for distant lions.

After a long build-up, Linda concluded: "You are the light of creation. Give thanks to nature. Allow the lions to give you a message. Now impart your own message back into the eco-system. Visualise the world as it should be. Rivers running pure and fresh, the land restored, animals with freedom to roam, all species given the right to flourish. Take this message from the lions back into the present. Come back, now, into your physical form, when you're ready."

The women around me opened their eyes. They were beaming with joy. Linda was also smiling broadly. "So, what did the lions say to you?" she asked.

The Austrian woman, close to tears, said, "They told to me: 'You have a plan, do it. Get on with it!'"

"That's wonderful," said Linda. "And you, Carla?"

"They tell me I am in the right place," said the tall

blonde. "I must continue doing the work I am doing."

"Yes, yes," said Linda. "The right place could mean so many things. Thank you for sharing."

The Swedish woman in the seat behind me was crying softly. "Agnetha, are you alright?"

"I... I cannot talk." She began sobbing. "I was in the legal, thinking world. I was sick. Now... better."

"Did you feel the light?" asked Linda in an encouraging tone.

"Yes, yes I think so."

"And you, Justin?"

"Ah, today I was just taking notes and watching the lions. Sorry, Linda."

She frowned. For a terrifying moment, I thought she was going to tell me to get off the vehicle and go sit with her cats. "Credo Mutwa tells us that Nature is magical and magic is natural. Never forget that!"

"Yes, Linda," I mumbled.

We drove back to the lodge in silence. Jason paused to let us watch the lioness Tswalu stalking a herd of zebras. They soon got wind of her and made off at a canter. "Perhaps the pyjama donkeys heard our thoughts and were alerted to Tswalu," suggested Linda.

Over breakfast, I asked Linda how she was able to maintain such a large and expensive operation without running a lodge for tourists. She acknowledged that it was indeed costly, with forty staff and a powerful anti-poaching unit. Donor funding was crucial, as well as the revenue from her leadership academy.

"The course is five intensive weeks, then counselling

for the rest of the year." She was addressing the volunteers as much as me. All of them were considering returning to Tsau to attend her course. "It's about finding your direction, being in balance with nature. It's about activating the lion heart in humanity. I define this as a quality of fearlessness inspired by love and reverence for nature. When you have that lion-heart quality, you are unstoppable.

"This is not the tradition presented to us by the figure of Hercules, the warrior who wanted a lion heart and slew the king of the beasts to get it. That's the egotistical, consumerist model. The end point of this kind of thinking is canned hunting, and ultimately the end of our planet's resources.

"At the leadership academy, we remind ourselves that there's another model to use as a prototype for humanity. It's about working with the lion as your friend. The figure we look at is Androcles, an escaped slave who encountered a lion with a thorn in its paw. Instead of being fearful, he removed the thorn. Later, Androcles was recaptured and thrown into an arena by the Romans to engage in mortal combat with a lion, which turned out to be the animal he'd saved. The emperor freed him after the lion refused to attack his friend.

"The Androcles model of lion-heartedness, just like Daniel in Judaism and Christianity, recognises that we are one with nature. Daniel could understand dreams. He had a vision of what humanity was like in the beginning. He said that the first beast was like a lion with wings, which stood on its hind legs and had a human heart.

That's what is being offered to us: the chance to reconnect with our lion heart and our higher potential.

"The leadership academy is very practical: we talk about how to reawaken those qualities and how to put them into action. We need to *celebrate* creation," Linda's eyes glowed. "We are part of the eco-system. When we get back to that understanding, we can help restore the eco-system as we restore ourselves."

Linda switched on her laptop and asked us to gather round. It showed a clip featuring Archbishop Emeritus Desmond Tutu's prayer for the white lions, recited in support of the global march for lions in 2014. The video started with sombre classical music and images of lions. "We pray that we may know that we are all created by You for abundance of life," intoned the Arch, "and that includes wildlife, and particularly at this time, we consider the risk faced by wild white lions. We thank You for those who make public this horrendous risk." Tutu's amen was punctuated by a lion roaring in full voice. All three volunteers were crying again.

Linda and Jason drove me to the airport. Maxi the Labrador saw us off at the gate. "With a haircut and a body shave that leave his mane and the tip of his tail shaggy, he could be even more terrifying," I said. "Especially at night."

"Good old Maxi couldn't hurt an ant," said Linda.

At Tsau's main gate, Jason checked the telemetry for lions once again. "We always have to be careful," he said. "Our cats are so precious. We've had poachers on the land, lions killed, snares set. Constant vigilance is essential."

At the airport, our farewells were surprisingly emotional. Perhaps all the tears were catching. Jason shook my hand, and Linda gave me a spirit-bear hug of lion-hearted proportions. She was formidable, no doubt about it. Her force of will carries this project she has made her life's work. A human lioness, a champion of the wild, a custodian of wilderness and of wild white lions. No matter the star stories, in the bigger scheme of things, I was in her camp. Long may she roar from her own Pride Rock in the heart of the African bush.

THIS FRAGILE ARK

I had come to the end of my quest and succeeded in finding four-and-a-half impossibles, which was more than an amateur like myself could rightly hope for. I would certainly be returning to the Cederberg to bag the other half of the Cape mountain leopard.

During my journey, I met a bunch of very special humans, many of whom had dedicated their lives to the creatures about which they felt so passionately. There was the insane Quinton Martins, who tramped the Cederberg for years and slept wild in search of his infuriating cats. There was Fred Dalerum, who jotted notes in ballpoint on his body during interminable desert hunts; Darren Pietersen attached backpacks to pangolins and kept road-kill in his freezer. Jolyon Neytzell-de-Wilde had left behind his city relationships and committed himself to the desert, and Shadrack Mkhabela had been attacked by a lioness, but refused to allow his partner to pull the trigger on her. And then there was Linda Tucker, who'd abandoned a high-flying career in Europe to try to save the white lions.

Let's not forget the tireless volunteers, people like Garth and Lorraine, who gave up their spare time to sit beside a leopard-trap receiver waiting for the signal to change, egged on by a fascist macaw. So too the anti-poaching trackers, who walked fifty kilometres a day in the good fight against stupidity and greed. There were the financial backers, like Cederberg farmer Johan van der Westhuizen, who'd given Quinton his first cheque to set up the Cape Leopard Trust, and benefactors such as the Oppenheimers of Tswalu and the head honchos at De Beers whose gift of Benfontein Farm provided an ideal research environment, as well as the many foreign donors who kept Linda's operation afloat. Then there were organisations such as EWT, CapeNature and SANParks that made conservation happen on an even larger scale.

Much serious science and wildlife management was being done behind the scenes of all these operations: genetic research, relocation of endangered species, studies of human-animal conflict, education programmes, diet analysis and negotiating with land owners to alter their practices and allow a bit of space on their farms and in their hearts for aardvark or leopard or pangolin.

Among these scientists, I sensed a hunger to understand how their respective environments worked, how each nut and bolt of the beautiful, complicated, godly system fitted together. Their research entailed methods both arduous and strange, like training dogs to chase (but not bite) the rarest of rabbits, playing Celine Dion to unsuspecting antelope or trying to arouse black-footed cats into ejaculation without the benefit of red roses and Champagne.

And then there were the poo fetishists. How many hours, days, weeks had these folk spent in the company of faeces? Soaking it in formalin, washing it, sifting it, separating the gorgeous titbits for close analysis, oven-baking it, showing it off to guests, who knows?

Tireless patience was also a hallmark of them all. Quinton went for months without glimpsing a leopard. Charmaine Theron spent countless hours giving termites yellow hairdos and then filming their gladiatorial antics. Keir and Darren hunted all night, every night, for rabbit and pangolin. It took Linda years to secure the land that would become a sanctuary for her white lions. Theirs is a very special brand of dedication.

I was moved by the reverence shown by my chaperones towards nature in all its forms. They would remain at respectful distances from animals, avoid crushing plants with their tyres, communicate their lack of threat to the creature in whatever way they could. Where violence of one form or another was required—through trapping, darting, relocation, or the like—their behaviour was like that of a doctor towards a beloved patient. The least amount of harm for the greatest scientific good was the manifest philosophy.

Each of my guides was an expert tracker. Like a child, I was learning a whole new language, one that scored the sand in a range of exquisite fonts. I marvelled at how easily my guides could identify spoor, even at night in tall grass, even after rain. Tracking was, of course, far more than following a set of prints. It involved reading the landscape and the wind, using eyes, nose and ears. What are those ants doing, why is that Bateleur circling, is that a whiff of buffalo on the breeze, why have the weaver birds built their nests so high in the tree this season? It's all about listening carefully to what the environment is telling you.

The best trackers were able to identify with their quarries and thereby predict their movements. They could climb inside the skin of the animal, turning themselves inside out, displaying their primal hides. Like characters from a fairy-tale, they became the creature. Quinton was a man-leopard who, in my eyes, grew whiskers and spots: he was to all intents and purposes already part feline. Fred wasn't a pathological urinater, but he certainly displayed the industry and tenacity of an aardwolf. Darren had become nocturnal and taken to tasting bitter ants to get closer to his totem, Keir's beard had turned the same hue as his piratical rabbits' ears, and I'd already begun to think of Linda as more lion than human.

Such identification with animals is a powerful form of empathy that most children instinctively understand. Furthermore, the auras that Linda spoke about, and her apparent ability to communicate with lions, all have their roots in theories about mind fields and the play of atoms around and within us that allow creatures to converse in invisible ways. Communication is certainly happening all around us at a more profound level than most of us are aware. Perhaps those big snowy cats had been chatting to me in lionese.

I learnt, too, about balance. How exterminating a "problem animal", like a leopard with a sheep tooth, could upset the ecological apple cart. Shooting dominant male lions takes out the best genes, and does untold harm to the pride. Aardvarks are crucial to the health of an eco-system and their discarded burrows provide homes for many other creatures. Every animal has its place.

Each of my five 'impossibles' had touched me in a particular way. I found myself both delighted and awestruck in their presence. There was the adorable, ghostly aardvark, shuffling through the tall Kalahari grass; the armour-plated pangolin clicking across a primordial dunescape like a mini World War I tank; a bunny with the widest grin you ever did see, bounding through the starlit fynbos; and a pair of colossal white cats that were, if not star beasts, then certainly superstars in their own right. And then there was the slinky she-leopard called Spot, who was or wasn't spotted, but who I could picture in my mind's eye as clear and present as a Wonderland dream. I recognised each of my creatures as being utterly in tune with the terrain they'd occupied for millions of years. The system was... they were... perfect.

The Impossible Five had become my very own umbrella species. I could use them as symbols for the eco-systems they inhabited. They stood for our wild lands, under constant threat and shrinking by the day. The Cederberg and Little Karoo with their sandstone mountains and tea-coloured streams, ancient rock art and fynbos treasuries; the Kalahari's scarlet dunes and pale grasslands dotted with camelthorn trees; the sweltering lowveld, piled high with thunderclouds, thick with leadwoods and limey fever trees, cut by sand rivers and teeming with big game. These sublime landscapes had entered my bloodstream.

There have been gains and losses in the fight to preserve my impossibles and their territories. In the Cederberg, where the greatest leopard-farmer conflict used to occur, there is now relative harmony, and many land owners have switched from livestock farming to cultivation. Vast nature reserves such as Tswalu and Sanbona have restored degraded farmlands to something of their original splendour, helping to give animals like the riverine rabbit a chance of survival. New reserves such as Tsau are doing pioneering work on lion conservation.

Elsewhere, the situation is more compromised and in unprotected areas the fate of endangered animals is in the hands of owners and land users. Ever-present are the threats of habitat loss, river contamination, the muti trade, canned hunting and the menace of the Far East with its insatiable hunger for body parts, horns, "raw materials": the very soul of our land.

My guides conveyed the importance of conservation in warrior terms. They spoke of the arrogance of humankind, overpopulation, climate change and the need for new political and economic systems that supersede today's growth models and put the Earth first. They warned of coming wars over natural resources such as water, and the necessity of fundamental changes in farming methods, to bring greater yields from smaller parcels of land. In essence, they all underlined the need for us to start thinking in radical new ways about our planet.

Perhaps Linda was right when she said that the pedantic intellectualism and cynicism of the pragmatists would not get us there. These revolutionary changes need the courageous, the audacious and the soulful.

In his book *Ecological Intelligence*, Ian McCallum talks of restoring Earth's "soul places", whose absence from our lives causes a form of homesickness. These are the wild lands that fill us with wonder and heal both the ills of our bodies and the loneliness of our souls. The destruction wreaked by humans on such places has been immense: whole eco-systems have collapsed. As Linda pointed out, we have broken our contract with nature, taking without giving back. Canned hunting for trophies is the symbolic antithesis of the relationship we need to engender with nature. It is up to us to restore that ancient pact, to heal the divide that has grown up between us and our planet.

With the deciphering of the human genome and the realisation that more than ninety percent of it is shared with all other mammals, we have been taken down a notch or two as a species. We can no longer see ourselves as the tip of the evolutionary spear. Indeed, we are but an upstart leaf on the branch of a very big, very old tree.

We are part of nature and it is part of us. Everything about our species, from the shape of our teeth to the size of our brains, has been fashioned over millennia by our interaction with the plants and animals around us. What's more, our sense of beauty and our greatest artistic achievements have been crafted in response to nature. Our yearning for wilderness is a hankering after the place we have come from, and from which we have become alienated in the headlong march of so-called progress.

McCallum writes further that the cure for this homesickness is "to remember that the wild areas of the world are the landscapes of the soul and that the creatures who belong there are soul-makers." Just as the ancient Celts needed their sacred groves, we need the wilderness "for that compulsive union of fact and feeling that we experience when we go there." Our very identity is tied to such places and their creatures, and we are dependent on them for our psychological health. The instinctive desire to protect endangered animals has at its core an implicit understanding that their fate is linked to ours and saving them is a step towards our own healing.

During my journey, I was repeatedly urged to open my eyes to nature's diverse wonderland, the barking geckos and shongololos, the mesembs and succulents—to value every individual animal and plant in the eco-system. Beyond my Impossible Five, there were millions of creatures even more impossibly impossible. It's estimated that seventy percent of the world's living species have yet to be identified. The great tragedy is that many of these will have been driven to extinction before they are even "discovered". Humans are responsible for the permanent disappearance of hundreds of plant and animal species each year. The scientists and conservationists I met are the brave gunslingers standing at the swing-doors of extinction.

The end result of our current path is the extinction of *Homo sapiens*. It is imperative that we cherish and protect wild places and the creatures they harbour. To harm them is to harm ourselves. All of us are sailing through space together on the same fragile, leaky ark. We are dependent on our shipmates for far more than their meat and hides, their horns and scales. Both our continued existence, and the wellbeing of our souls, hinge on the complex matrix of life around us.

We must affirm that the wilderness is not for sale. Its creatures are not commodities, and must never be viewed as mere "natural resources". Even a single pangolin scale should be treasured. Each one is, in fact, priceless.

SELECT BIBLIOGRAPHY

Adams, D. and Carwardine, M. *Last Chance to See* (Pan Books, London, 1990).

Adams, R. *Watership Down* (Rex Collins, London, 1972).

Apps, P. Smither's *Mammals of Southern Africa: A Field Guide* (Struik, Cape Town, 2012).

Carroll, L. *The Complete Stories and Poems of Lewis Carroll* (Geddes & Grosset, New Lanark, 2002).

Chatwin, B. *The Songlines* (Picador, London, 1987).

Collins, K. *Habitat Availability for the Riverine Rabbit, Bunolagus Monticularis* (unpublished MSc thesis, University of Pretoria, 2001).

Cullinan, C. *Wild Law: Governing People for Earth* (Siber Ink, Cape Town, 2002).

Daly, R. "What Goes Bump in the Night?" in *Getaway*, August 2001, 44–47.

De Vries, J. L., Pirk, C. W. W., Bateman, P. W., Cameron, E. Z. and Dalerum, F. "Extension of the Diet of an Extreme Foraging Specialist, the Aardwolf (*Proteles cristata*)", *African Zoology* Vol 46, No 1, April 2011, 194–196.

Frandsen, R. *Southern Africa's Mammals: A Field Guide* (Frandsen Publishers, Johannesburg, 1995).

Ganswindt, A., Parys, A., Wielebnowski, N. and Lehmann, T. "Non-Invasive Assessment of Reproductive and Adrenocortical Steroid Hormones in Captive Aardvarks (Orycteropus Afer)", *Afrotherian Conservation* No 8 (June 2011), 17–18.

Hughs, G. O., Thuiller, W., Midgley, G. F. and Collins, K. "Environmental Change Hastens the Demise of the Critically Endangered Riverine Rabbit (*Bunolagus monticularis*)", *Biological Conservation* No 141 (2008).

Kosová, M. and Stanovsky, V. (eds). *African Tales of Magic and Mystery* (Hamlyn, London, 1970).

Lynch, K. *Bunolagus Monticularis: Riverine Rabbit Monitoring Program* (Sanbona Wildlife Reserve publication, Sanbona, 2009).

Maskew, M. *A Portrait of Uys Krige* (Chelsea Gallery, Wynberg, 1985).

Matthiessen, P. *The Snow Leopard* (Penguin, New York, 1987).

McBride, C. *The White Lions of Timbavati* (Paddington Press, New York, 1977).

McCallum, I. *Ecological Intelligence: Rediscovering Ourselves in Nature* (Africa Geographic, Cape Town, 2005).

Milne, A. A. *The House at Pooh Corner* (Methuen, London, 1953).

Milne, A. A. *Winnie-the-Pooh* (Methuen, London, 1953).

Potter, B. *The Complete Tales of Beatrix Potter* (Frederick Warne, London, 1989).

Tucker, L. *Mystery of the White Lions: Children of the Sun God* (Hay House, London, 2010).

Tucker, L. *Saving the White Lions: One Woman's Battle for Africa's Most Sacred Animal* (North Atlantic Books, Berkeley, 2013).

Watson, S. *Return of the Moon: Versions from the /Xam* (Carrefour, Cape Town, 1991).

Many juicy morsels of information were also scavenged from internet sites such as those of Cape Leopard Trust, De Beers, Endangered Wildlife Trust, Global White Lion Protection Trust, Motswari, Sanbona and Tswalu.

ABOUT THE AUTHOR

Justin Fox is a travel writer and photographer. Fox was a Rhodes Scholar and received a doctorate in English from Brasenose College, Oxford University. He was a research fellow at the University of Cape Town, where he now teaches part-time. He is a two-time Mondi journalism award winner and his articles have appeared internationally in a wide range of publications, while his short stories and poems have been published in various anthologies.

useful for ... reproduction and photographic reproduction. ... Editor authors share a common set of ... from Document Delivery. ... Much of it is drawn from knowledge of the full life cycle of a particular publication or low-budget document ... set for researching. Much is learned and has evolved and has produced a standard publication ... journal, magazine, book, manual, bulletin, booklet, short article and photo ... have been published in various ... and formats.